DEFENSE, SECURITY AND STRATEGIES



# COUNTERFEIT PARTS IN THE DEPARTMENT OF DEFENSE SUPPLY CHAIN

## REPORTING CHALLENGES AND RISK ISSUES

# DEFENSE, SECURITY AND STRATEGIES

Additional books in this series can be found on Nova's website under the Series tab.

Additional e-books in this series can be found on Nova's website under the eBooks tab.

DEFENSE, SECURITY AND STRATEGIES

# COUNTERFEIT PARTS IN THE DEPARTMENT OF DEFENSE SUPPLY CHAIN

## REPORTING CHALLENGES AND RISK ISSUES

ERIK DAWSON
EDITOR

*New York*

**Library of Congress Cataloging-in-Publication Data**

ISBN: 978-1-63485-989-9

*Published by Nova Science Publishers, Inc. † New York*

# CONTENTS

# PREFACE

The Department of Defense (DOD) supply chain is vulnerable to the risk of counterfeit parts, which have the potential to delay missions and ultimately endanger service members. To effectively identify and mitigate this risk, DOD began requiring its agencies in 2013 and its contractors in 2014, to report data on suspect counterfeit parts. This book examines, among other things, the use of the Government-Industry Data Exchange Program (GIDEP) to report counterfeits; GIDEP's effectiveness as an early warning system; and DOD's assessment of defense contractors' systems for detecting and avoiding counterfeits.

In: Counterfeit Parts
Editor: Erik Dawson
ISBN: 978-1-63485-989-9


*Chapter 1*

# COUNTERFEIT PARTS: DOD NEEDS TO IMPROVE REPORTING AND OVERSIGHT TO REDUCE SUPPLY CHAIN RISK*

***United States Government Accountability Office***

## WHY GAO DID THIS STUDY

The DOD supply chain is vulnerable to the risk of counterfeit parts, which have the potential to delay missions and ultimately endanger service members. To effectively identify and mitigate this risk, DOD began requiring its agencies in 2013 and its contractors in 2014, to report data on suspect counterfeit parts. A Senate report included a provision for GAO to review DOD's efforts to secure its supply chain from counterfeit parts. This report examines, among other things, (1) the use of GIDEP to report counterfeits, (2) GIDEP's effectiveness as an early warning system, and (3) DOD's assessment of defense contractors' systems for detecting and avoiding counterfeits.

GAO analyzed data from GIDEP for fiscal years 2011 through 2015; reviewed DOD policies, procedures, and documents; and met with agency officials and seven selected contractors based on dollar value from contracts that included a new counterfeit clause.

---

* This is an edited, reformatted and augmented version of a United States Government Accountability Office, Publication No. GAO-16-236, dated February 2016.

## What GAO Recommends

GAO recommends that DOD oversee its defense agencies' reporting efforts, develop standard processes for when to report a part as suspect counterfeit, establish guidance for when to limit access tor GIDEP reports, and clarify criteria to contractors for their detection systems. DOD agreed with the 3 recommendations on GIDEP reporting but partially agreed with the recommendation to clarify criteria, stating it did not agree with providing specific implementation details. GAO continues to believe clarifying criteria is important, which is different than specific implementation details.

## What GAO Found

Department of Defense (DOD) agencies and contractors submitted 526 suspect counterfeit parts reports in the Government-Industry Data Exchange Program (GIDEP) from fiscal years 2011 through 2015, submitted primarily by contractors. Defense agencies and contractor officials explained that congressional attention to counterfeit parts in 2011 and 2012 led to increased reporting, and that the lower number of reports in more recent years is partly the result of better practices to prevent the purchase of counterfeit parts.

Several aspects of DOD's implementation of its mandatory GIDEP reporting for suspect counterfeit parts have limited GIDEP's effectiveness as an early warning system.

- First, DOD is not conducting oversight to ensure that defense agencies are reporting as required. As a result, the Defense Logistics Agency (DLA), for example, may be underreporting suspect counterfeit parts in GIDEP.
- Second, there is no standardized process for establishing how much evidence is needed before reporting suspect counterfeit parts in GIDEP and DLA applies a significantly more stringent standard than, for example, the Navy. Consequently, reports may not be submitted in a timely manner.
- Third, defense agencies typically limit access of suspect counterfeit GIDEP reports to government agencies, so industry is not aware of the potential counterfeiting issues identified. DOD policy does not

include guidance about when access to these reports should be limited.

All seven contractors GAO spoke with have established systems to detect and avoid counterfeit electronic parts; however, DOD has not finalized how these systems will be assessed. Contractors are seeking additional clarification on how to meet some of DOD's requirements. Until DOD clarifies criteria for contractors on how their systems will be evaluated, it cannot fully ensure these systems detect and avoid electronic counterfeit parts, as required.

## ABBREVIATIONS LIST

| | |
|---|---|
| DCMA | Defense Contract Management Agency |
| DFARS | Defense Federal Acquisition Regulation Supplement |
| DLA | Defense Logistics Agency |
| DOD | Department of Defense |
| FAR | Federal Acquisition Regulation |
| GIDEP | Government-Industry Data Exchange Program |
| MDA | Missile Defense Agency |
| NASA | National Aeronautics and Space Administration |
| PDREP | Product Data Reporting and Evaluation Program |
| USD AT&L | Under Secretary of Defense for Acquisition, Technology, and Logistics |

* * *

February 16, 2016

Congressional Committees

The Department of Defense (DOD) draws from a large network of global suppliers and, in fiscal year 2014, managed over 4.7 million parts that are used in, for example, communication and weapon systems, at a cost of over $96 billion. The existence of counterfeit parts in the DOD supply chain can, for example, delay missions, affect the integrity of systems, and ultimately endanger the lives of service members. Almost anything is at risk of being counterfeited, including microelectronics used in fighter jets and missile guidance systems, fasteners used in aircraft, and materials used in engine mounts. In response to this risk, in 2013, DOD created a Counterfeit Prevention Policy for department-wide action to mitigate the risk of counterfeit parts, which included steps to prevent the introduction of counterfeit materials into the supply chain, as well as testing and other means by which to detect materials that may have already entered it. DOD also issued regulations, as required by the 2012 National Defense Authorization Act, requiring that its personnel and contractors report suspected counterfeit electronic parts to a cooperative activity between government and industry for sharing technical information called the Government-Industry Data Exchange Program (GIDEP)—a program that allows government and industry participants to share information on nonconforming parts, including suspect counterfeit parts, via a web-based database—and that contractors develop and maintain systems to detect and avoid counterfeit electronic parts.

Congress has raised questions about DOD's ability to secure the supply chain and report on counterfeit or suspect counterfeit parts. The Senate Armed Services Committee report accompanying a bill for the National Defense Authorization Act for Fiscal Year 2015 included a provision for GAO to review DOD's efforts to address vulnerabilities to counterfeit parts in its supply chain.[1] This report determines (1) the use of GIDEP to report suspect counterfeit parts, from fiscal years 2011 through 2015; (2) the effectiveness of GIDEP reporting as an early warning system for counterfeit parts; (3) the extent to which DOD has assessed defense contractors' systems for detecting and avoiding counterfeit parts; and (4) key ongoing efforts by selected government and industry organizations to improve the detection and reporting of counterfeit or suspect counterfeit parts.

To do this work, we examined laws and regulations regarding counterfeit parts, including section 818 of the 2012 National Defense Authorization Act, the Federal Acquisition Regulation (FAR) and the Defense Federal Acquisition Regulation Supplement (DFARS), as well as reviewed DOD counterfeit prevention policies and guidance relating to detecting and avoiding counterfeit parts. We reviewed the guidance on reporting counterfeit parts from the military services (the Departments of the Army, Air Force, and Navy) as well as from the Defense Contract Management Agency (DCMA), Defense Logistics Agency (DLA), and Missile Defense Agency (MDA) and interviewed officials about relevant policies and practices. We also analyzed data from GIDEP and the Product Data Reporting and Evaluation Program (PDREP) to determine the extent and limitations in reporting suspect and confirmed counterfeit parts for fiscal years 2011 through 2015. After interviewing GIDEP program officials and reviewing the entire GIDEP database and related documents, we determined that the data was sufficiently reliable for the purposes of this report. We selected seven contractors by identifying the top five prime contractors based on dollar value from contracts containing the 2014 DFARS clause for counterfeit detection and avoidance, as well as two additional major prime contractors. From each, we reviewed one sample contract as well as selected contractor procedures and systems for detecting and avoiding counterfeit parts; and identified and evaluated DOD's systems for monitoring contractor compliance with related regulations. We reviewed documents and met with officials from other selected federal agencies, such as the Department of Homeland Security and the National Aeronautics and Space Administration (NASA); as well as organizations including SAE International, Aerospace Industries Association, and the Independent Distributors of Electronics Association to obtain information about efforts to detect and avoid counterfeit parts. We visited DLA's Land and Maritime Division in Columbus, Ohio; where the agency maintains an electronic testing facility and an authentication program for microcircuits, and the product testing facilities at the Naval Surface Warfare Center in Crane, Indiana. We assessed DOD's policies, procedures and practices against criteria in *Standards for Internal Control in the Federal Government*.[2] Appendix I provides a more detailed description of our scope and methodology.

We conducted this performance audit from January 2015 to February 2016 in accordance with generally accepted government auditing standards. Those standards require that we plan and perform the audit to obtain sufficient, appropriate evidence to provide a reasonable basis for our findings and conclusions based on our audit objectives. We believe that the evidence obtained provides a reasonable basis for our findings and conclusions based on our audit objectives.

## BACKGROUND

DOD draws from a large number of suppliers in a global supply chain—in both the acquisition phase and throughout a system's operational and sustainment phases—providing multiple opportunities for the risk of counterfeit parts into these systems. DOD contractors rely on thousands of subcontractors and suppliers, including the original component manufacturers that assemble microcircuits and the mid-level manufacturers subcontracted to develop the individual subsystems that make up a complete system or supply. Once contractors deliver a system to the military services, DLA can play a critical role in its sustainment. For example, DLA is primarily responsible for logistical support for more than 2,400 weapon systems across the military services. As part of its sustainment functions, DLA provides approximately 90 percent of the military's repair parts. Also, as systems age, products required to support them may no longer be available from original component manufacturers, original equipment manufacturers or their authorized distributors. These products could be available from independent distributors, brokers, or aftermarket manufacturers; but these suppliers often have less traceability to the original source. DOD has adopted industry standards and continues to participate in government and industry groups that develop international standards for the aerospace and automotive industry, such as the SAE International's G-19 Committee. Specifically, in 2009 DOD adopted SAE International's Aerospace Standard 5553 Counterfeit Electronic Parts: Avoidance, Detection, Mitigation and Disposition (AS5553) that includes definitions of the sources of supply for parts, and associated risk, which was updated in 2013 (as shown in figure 1).

| ◀ Lower risk | | | Higher risk ▶ |
|---|---|---|---|
| **Original component manufacturer**<br>Entity that designs and/or engineers a part and is pursuing or has obtained the intellectual property rights to that part. | **Authorized supplier**<br>Includes aftermarket manufacturers or suppliers of a part authorized by the original component manufacturer, such a franchised distributor;<br>• Aftermarket manufacturer: Manufacturer that is authorized by the original component manufacturer to produce and sell replacement parts, usually due to an original component manufacturer decision to discontinue production of a part, and/or produces parts that meet or match specifications without violating the original component manufacturer's intellectual property rights.<br>• Franchised (authorized) distributor: entity that distributes products within the terms of an original component manufacturer contractual agreement.<br>Note: Some authorized suppliers will provide other services which are not authorized by the original component manufacturer. | **Original equipment manufacturer**<br>Company that manufactures products it has designed from purchased components and sells those products under the company's brand name. These are generally prime contractors or high-level subcontractors. | **Independent distributor**<br>Distributor that purchases parts with the intention to sell and redistribute them back into the market and do not normally have contractual agreements or obligations with original component manufacturers. This includes brokers who work in a "just-in-time" environment by searching the industry and locating parts for customers. |

Source: GAO Summary of SAE International, AS5553A, Fraudulent/Counterfeit Electronic Parts Avoidance, Detection, Mitigation, and Disposition. Revised January 2013. | GAO-16-236.

Figure 1. DOD Sources of Supply and Risk According to SAE Aerospace Standard 5553.

According to DLA officials, DLA does not use AS5553 because it is generally applied to system integrators, but uses other aerospace standards to govern its procurement of microelectronic parts from individual suppliers.[3] These standards emphasize the importance of purchasing parts from original component manufacturers or authorized suppliers—when available—as the most effective method to avoid counterfeit parts. If purchasing a part from an independent distributor is necessary, the buyer should consider applying additional counterfeit mitigation methods, such as testing for product verification, based on the risk of the supplier and criticality of the part.

Over the past 6 years, GAO, Congress, and the Department of Commerce have issued reports on the existence of counterfeit parts in the DOD supply chain. In three reports since 2010, we have identified risks and challenges associated with counterfeit parts and counterfeit prevention at both DOD and NASA, including inconsistent definitions of counterfeit parts and poorly targeted quality control practices, as well as potential barriers to improvements to these practices.[4] In 2012, we created a fictitious company, and through it were able to report on the availability of suspect counterfeit electronic parts available for purchase from companies selling military-grade parts on the Internet. In our prior reports, we made a total of five recommendations for improvements. DOD has taken action to implement three of these recommendations, but neither DOD nor NASA have yet implemented the remaining two recommendations: on tracking the frequency with which parts with quality issues, including counterfeit parts, make their way into the supply chain; and on making that information available to Congress. In 2012, Senate investigators reported that approximately 1,800 instances of suspect counterfeit parts were identified by DLA, defense contractors and testers in the 2-year period from 2009 to 2010—before reporting suspect counterfeit parts in GIDEP became mandatory—and that the vast majority of those cases appeared to have gone unreported to DOD or criminal authorities.[5]

To enhance DOD's efforts to detect and avoid counterfeit electronic parts, Section 818 of the 2012 National Defense Authorization Act directed DOD to define suspect and confirmed counterfeit electronic parts, implement a risk-based approach to mitigate the risk of counterfeit electronic parts, and use GIDEP to report counterfeit incidents.[6] It also included specific sections pertaining to DOD's supply chain—requiring certain DOD contractors to enhance their systems to detect and avoid counterfeit electronic parts, and to report all counterfeit and suspect counterfeit electronic parts in GIDEP within 60 days.[7] Finally, Section 818 required DOD to revise DFARS so that costs of rework or corrective action associated with a counterfeit electronic part supplied by certain contractors are not allowable under DOD contracts.[8] Figure 2 shows the timeline of congressional and DOD actions relating to counterfeit parts from 2011 to 2014.

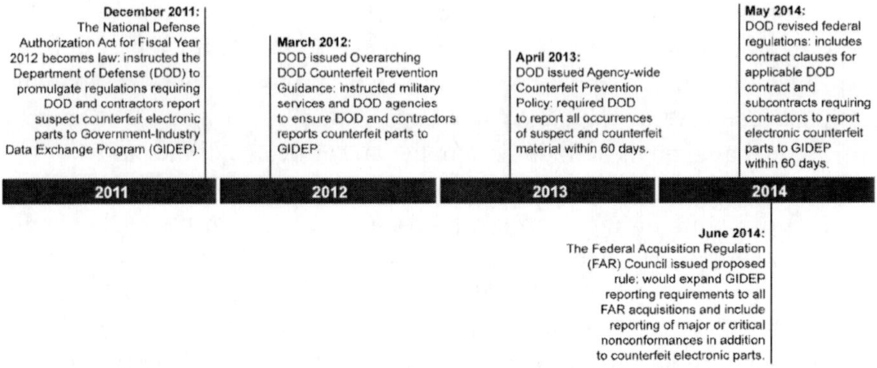


Source: PL 112-81, § 818; Memorandum for Secretaries of the Military Departments and Directors of the Defense Agencies, Overarching DOD Counterfeit Prevention Guidance (March 16, 2012); DODI 4140.67; 79 Federal Register 26092 (May 6, 2014); 79 Federal Register 33164 (June 10, 2014) | GAO-16-236

Figure 2. Timeline of Federal Actions Related to GIDEP Reporting of Counterfeit Parts.

DOD issued its Counterfeit Prevention Policy in April 2013. The policy aims to 1) prevent the introduction of counterfeit materiel at any level of the DOD supply chain, including electronic parts; and 2) provide direction for anti-counterfeit measures for DOD weapon and information systems acquisition and sustainment to prevent the introduction of counterfeit materiel.[9] While the instructions in Section 818 to DOD are specifically applied to counterfeit electronic parts, the policy applies to all counterfeit materiel, not just electronic parts. DOD's Counterfeit Prevention Policy provides the following definitions for counterfeit items:

- Counterfeit materiel: an item that is an unauthorized copy or substitute that has been identified, marked, or altered by a source other than the item's legally authorized source and has been misrepresented to be an authorized item of the legally authorized source.
- Suspect counterfeit: materiel, items, or products in which there is an indication by visual inspection, testing, or other information that it may meet the definition of counterfeit materiel.

The Counterfeit Prevention Policy established roles and responsibilities for implementing DOD's anti-counterfeiting strategy as well as GIDEP reporting for counterfeit parts. Three offices within the Under Secretary of Defense for Acquisition, Technology, and Logistics (USD AT&L) have primary responsibility for counterfeit parts. First, the Assistant Secretary of Defense for Logistics and Materiel Readiness is designated as the primary point of contact office with the primary responsibility to implement, monitor, and continually develop DOD's anti-counterfeit strategy. Second, the Assistant Secretary of Defense for Research and Engineering, among other responsibilities, acts as the principal point of contact for GIDEP and is to determine and implement enhancements to GIDEP to expand its usefulness and robustness in anti-counterfeiting efforts in the DOD supply chain. Finally, the Director of Defense Procurement, Acquisition Policy, and Strategic Sourcing develops and modifies procurement policies, procedures, regulations, and guidance to support DOD's Counterfeit Prevention Policy.

DOD's Counterfeit Prevention Policy requires DOD component heads to report all occurrences of suspect and confirmed counterfeit parts in GIDEP, DOD's central reporting repository for suspect or confirmed counterfeit parts. Managed by DOD's Defense Standardization Program Office, GIDEP manages a web-based program that allows government and industry participants to share information on nonconforming parts, including but not limited to counterfeit parts (confirmed and suspected). Other types of information reported by GIDEP includes notices for when production of a part is about to be discontinued or when the attributes of parts, components, or materials have been changed by a manufacturer. A part that is found to be nonconforming is not necessarily counterfeit as counterfeit parts involve the intent to misrepresent the identity or pedigree of a part. DOD also uses the term "deficient" to have the same meaning as "nonconforming." The Policy requires the reporting of all occurrences of suspect and confirmed counterfeit materiel to (1) appropriate authorities, nonconformance reporting systems, and GIDEP within 60 calendar days; and (2) DOD criminal investigative organizations and other DOD law enforcement authorities at the earliest opportunity. It further states that when critical materiel is identified as suspect counterfeit, to expeditiously disseminate a notification to other DOD components to maintain weapon systems operational performance and preserve life or safety of operating personnel. According to several DOD officials we spoke with, GIDEP is intended to be an early warning system. DOD military services and components also use two other systems to report nonconforming parts—the Product Data Reporting and Evaluation Program

(PDREP) and the Joint Deficiency Reporting System.[10] In both systems, users can specifically categorize reported nonconforming parts as suspect counterfeit. As DOD's Counterfeit Prevention Policy mandates documenting all occurrences of suspect counterfeit parts in GIDEP, entries into these other systems do not fulfill the DOD reporting requirement. In May 2014, DOD revised the DFARS to require that contractors subject to cost accounting standards, when delivering electronic parts or supplies containing electronic parts, 1) report suspect and confirmed counterfeit electronic parts in GIDEP; and 2) have systems in place to detect and avoid counterfeit electronic parts. Additionally, the DFARS requires that prime contractors subject to the cost accounting standards flow down these requirements to their subcontractors, regardless of whether those subcontractors are subject to the cost accounting standards.[11] Prime contractors not subject to the cost accounting standards are not required to apply or flow down these requirements. The new counterfeit prevention policies supplement long-standing FAR contract quality requirements.[12]

## Defense Agencies and Contractors Are Submitting Fewer Counterfeit Parts Reports in GIDEP

Defense contractors and agencies are submitting counterfeit parts reports, but fewer reports have been submitted to GIDEP since DOD implemented its Counterfeit Prevention Policy and reporting requirements in 2013. For fiscal years 2011 through 2015, we found that 526 reports of suspect counterfeit parts were entered in GIDEP, over 90 percent of which were submitted by contractors.[13] Figure 3 shows the number of reports submitted by contractors and government agencies in each fiscal year.

Most of these reports were submitted in 2011 and 2012, when some DOD and contractor officials we spoke with said that congressional attention to counterfeit parts prompted contractors to examine their inventory and identify previously undetected counterfeit parts. In addition, there was an amnesty period in early fiscal year 2011 when suspect counterfeit parts reports could be submitted without naming a supplier, which DOD officials said led to temporarily increased reporting, mostly from distributors who have submitted few reports since. In more recent years, defense agencies and contractors we met with stated that they have encountered counterfeit parts less frequently in the DOD supply chain, in part, because they are applying more stringent standards about which independent distributors they rely on for parts that cannot be acquired directly from the original manufacturer.

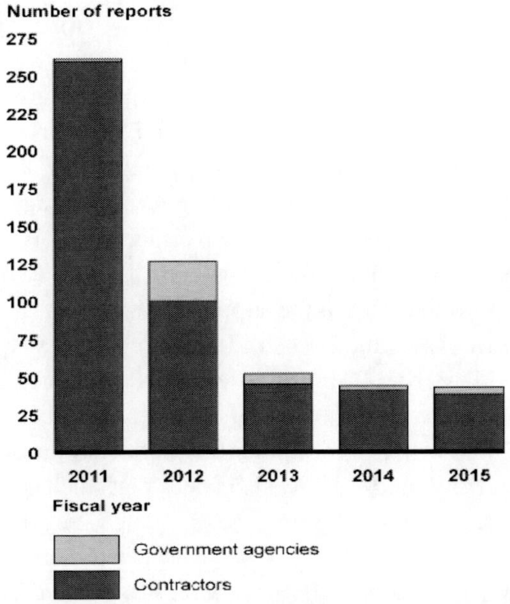


Source: GAO analysis of Government-Industry Data Exchange Program data. | GAO-16-236.

Figure 3. Number of Government-Industry Data Exchange Program Suspect Counterfeit Reports for Fiscal Years 2011 – 2015.

While the names of the suppliers can be identified in GIDEP reports, almost half of 526 GIDEP reports in our analysis did not include the name of the supplier for the parts in question. Further, the reports do not always indicate the original source from whom the supplier purchased the counterfeit part, which could be further down the supply chain and may or may not be known by the entity submitting the report. At our request, GIDEP staff categorized the suppliers identified in counterfeit parts reports issued in fiscal years 2011 through 2015 by their role in the supply chain, based on their personal knowledge and industry expertise, and we conducted analysis based on these classifications.[14] In the 296 reports that contained supplier information, 319 unique suppliers were named.[15] Of these, 88 percent were classified by GIDEP staff as independent distributors and 10 percent were classified as midlevel manufacturers. One independent distributor was named in 30 different GIDEP reports, all of which were submitted by one original equipment manufacturer within a 7-month period.

GIDEP staff also provided classifications for the entities that submitted GIDEP reports by their role in the supply chain, upon which we based our analysis. From fiscal years 2011 through 2015, we found that nearly 40 percent of suspect counterfeit parts reports—207 of 526—were submitted by independent distributors, with three companies submitting 103 reports. In addition, one-third of all suspect counterfeit GIDEP reports—178 of 526—were submitted by original equipment manufacturers, with 122 of these 178 reports submitted by two manufacturers, while government agencies submitted only 43 reports. DOD submitted 40 of 43 government reports, with the Navy submitting more than half of these. See appendix II for additional details of reports by role of reporting entity in the supply chain.

The Army, the Air Force and MDA did not submit any suspect counterfeit GIDEP reports in this period. Air Force officials explained that they have relied on their contractors to submit reports because they have the best knowledge of how and where the counterfeit part was procured. Similarly, officials from the Army and MDA also said that their contractors have submitted suspect counterfeit GIDEP reports related to parts procured for Army and MDA products. Specifically, MDA officials said that their contractors submitted five of the GIDEP reports we reviewed, some of which involved parts detected due to concerns raised by MDA. DLA officials also noted that they encourage contractors and subcontractors to submit reports when counterfeit parts are encountered. However, according to DOD officials, most of DLA's contractors are not large enough to follow cost accounting standards and therefore are not bound by the GIDEP reporting requirement in the DFARS. To address this, defense officials stated that DLA requires any company participating in one of its qualified supplier programs to report in GIDEP.

## Aspects of Implementation Have Limited GIDEP's Effectiveness as an Early Warning System for Counterfeit Parts

Several aspects of DOD's implementation of its mandatory reporting requirement for suspect counterfeit parts in GIDEP have limited GIDEP's effectiveness as an early warning system to prevent counterfeit parts from entering the defense supply chain. First, DOD has not established an oversight function to ensure that defense agencies are reporting suspect counterfeit parts as required. As a result, for example, reporting practices at DLA do not conform to either DOD- or DLA-level reporting policies and it is likely that DLA is not reporting all of the suspect counterfeit parts detected in GIDEP as suspect counterfeit parts. Second, there is not a standardized process for establishing how much evidence is needed before reporting suspect counterfeit parts in GIDEP. We found that defense agencies and contractors have used different practices for determining when to report a part as suspect counterfeit and DLA applies a significantly more stringent standard than other defense agencies and contractors we reviewed. As a result, reports may not be submitted in a timely manner. Third, defense agencies typically limit access of suspect counterfeit GIDEP reports to government agencies, so industry is not aware of the potential counterfeiting issues identified. DOD's Counterfeit Prevention Policy does not include guidance about when limiting access to suspect counterfeit parts GIDEP reports is appropriate. *Standards for Internal Control in the Federal Government* call for information to be recorded and communicated to others, such as stakeholders who need it, to help the agency achieve its goals. These standards also state that control activities should be in place to help ensure that management's directives are carried out, such as ensuring completeness and accuracy of information processing.[16]

## Limited Department-Level Oversight Leads to Uncertainty about Completeness of GIDEP Reporting

DOD has not provided adequate department-level oversight to ensure that all defense agencies are reporting in GIDEP as required and, as a result, it is likely that defense agencies—particularly DLA—are not reporting all of the suspect counterfeit parts they detect in GIDEP as suspect counterfeit. *Standards for Internal Control in the Federal Government* call for reviews by management at the functional or activity level to compare actual performance to planned or expected performance and analyze significant differences.[17] Completeness and timeliness of GIDEP reporting relies on DOD ensuring that reporting practices align with established Counterfeit Prevention Policy. According to a senior USD AT&L official, GIDEP staff do not play a role in overseeing and monitoring whether defense agencies and contractors are meeting reporting requirements. DOD policy does not provide for an oversight role to ensure that reporting of counterfeit parts is tracked. The senior USD

AT&L official explained that the department has taken a decentralized approach to implementing GIDEP reporting requirements, depending on the components to provide additional guidance and oversight. While defense agencies generally each have a central point person overseeing use of GIDEP, DOD does not oversee GIDEP reporting at a department-wide level. According to DOD's Counterfeit Prevention Policy, three entities within USD AT&L share responsibilities for DOD's anti-counterfeiting efforts. The senior USD AT&L official stated that certain GIDEP oversight functions, such as oversight of reporting by DOD agencies, may fall between the responsibilities of these organizations.

Moreover, defense officials have not analyzed or provided oversight of defense agencies' compliance with GIDEP reporting requirements, monitoring only whether agencies have established their own policies. A senior USD AT&L official responsible for counterfeit prevention policy we spoke with was not aware of DLA's low level of reporting and has not analyzed the reasons for it in light of DLA's central role in procuring parts for DOD. Specifically, this official said that USD AT&L has not conducted analysis that shows that DLA submitted very few reports in recent years. As a result of DOD's decentralized approach and lack of department-level oversight, the department cannot ensure that GIDEP data accurately reflect the extent to which suspect counterfeit parts have been identified by defense agencies.

DLA plays a central role in procuring parts to sustain existing weapon systems. Navy and Air Force officials we spoke with noted that they do not typically purchase parts directly from suppliers, so they would expect counterfeit parts to be reported by their defense contractors or DLA. However, DLA submitted only nine suspect counterfeit GIDEP reports in fiscal years 2011 through 2015, with none submitted in 2014 and just one in 2015. DLA officials described instances where parts were identified as potentially suspect counterfeit, but these were reported in GIDEP as nonconforming parts, not suspect counterfeit. While this step provides GIDEP users with notice that parts did not meet contract specifications and may present safety problems, it does not inform users about potential counterfeiting concerns.

In another example, in 2012, the Air Force did not report a debarred subcontractor in GIDEP for supplying counterfeit electronics components, even after the investigation was made public.[18] Although Air Force officials stated that its prime contractor submitted related suspect counterfeit GIDEP reports about some parts, these reports did not include the name of the debarred subcontractor; rather they listed only the independent distributor that the parts were sold through. Without a GIDEP report that included critical information about the original source of suspect counterfeit parts, other defense agencies and contractors may not have the information necessary to raise their awareness of the problem or to check whether other distributors also sold parts from that same source.

Further, DOD officials told us that not all suspect counterfeit parts that are reported to other data sources are reported in GIDEP as suspect counterfeit. Specifically, PDREP—the Navy's system for reporting supplier performance and quality information used across several defense agencies—allows the entity that submits a report about a nonconforming part to identify the part as suspect counterfeit. According to DOD policy, it is then the responsibility of a specific agency identified in PDREP to determine whether to report in GIDEP, which is possible through an automated function within PDREP. We found 268 PDREP reports labeled as suspect counterfeit parts by various DOD entities between October 2010 and August 2015.[19] However, only 10—or 4 percent—are clearly documented as having been reported in GIDEP. While defense agency and contractor officials explained that there are instances where an initial suspicion of counterfeiting is quickly proven incorrect, defense officials also stated that at least some parts identified in PDREP as potentially counterfeit should be reported in GIDEP but are not. Navy officials noted that this is particularly common when DLA is responsible for resolving the claims. For example, DLA created a parts quality report in PDREP, coded the parts report as suspect counterfeit, and tested the parts at its product testing and evaluation program. The parts failed visual and dimensional test requirements, but were not reported in GIDEP as suspect counterfeit. DLA was the agency responsible for determining whether to report in GIDEP for 148 of the 268 PDREP reports we reviewed that were labeled as suspect counterfeit. However, DLA submitted only one of the related GIDEP reports we identified.

In our review, we found that another source of information about suspect counterfeit parts and their suppliers, ERAI, had significantly more suspect counterfeit reports than GIDEP, further calling into question GIDEP's completeness. ERAI—a company that monitors, investigates and reports issues affecting the global electronics supply chain—provides paying members from government and industry with access to a database with reports of nonconforming parts and their suppliers. According to ERAI, most of its members are independent brokers, but also includes original equipment manufacturers and government users. According to ERAI's data its users report more suspect counterfeit parts than are reported in GIDEP. For example, from 2011 through 2015, over 4,000 reports of suspect counterfeit electrical, electronic, and electromechanical parts were submitted to ERAI, over 7 times the amount of suspect counterfeit reports for all types of parts submitted in GIDEP during the same period.[20] ERAI and agency officials largely attribute this high number to the fact that reports in ERAI are submitted anonymously. While ERAI includes reports about commercial and defense industry suppliers, an ERAI official noted that both sectors often rely on the same pool of suppliers.

## DOD Lacks a Standardized Process for Determining When to Report Suspect Counterfeit Parts in GIDEP

There is no standardized process for establishing how much evidence is needed before reporting suspect counterfeit parts in GIDEP, and DLA applies a more stringent standard than other defense agencies and contractors we reviewed. When suspect counterfeit parts are discovered, we found that defense agencies and contractors generally take additional steps to establish reasonable certainty that parts are counterfeit before submitting suspect counterfeit GIDEP reports, although practices for making this determination differ and therefore take varying amounts of time. We found that some of the defense agencies and contractors we reviewed have practices for reporting parts as suspect counterfeit in GIDEP within the 60-day reporting period, but that DLA's practices can take significantly longer to complete.

According to the GIDEP operations manual, reports should be submitted no more than 60 days from the time of discovery to preclude further loss to government and industry users. In addition, the objective of GIDEP reports, including suspect counterfeit parts reports, is to preclude the integration of these items into government and industry systems and inventory.[21] Moreover, DOD's 2013 Counterfeit Prevention Policy states that it is DOD's policy to make information about counterfeiting accessible at all levels of the DOD supply chain as a method to prevent further counterfeiting.[22] DOD and industry officials noted that timely reporting of suspect counterfeit parts to GIDEP is critical to using the system as an early warning system. For example, one USD AT&L official stated that DOD's goal for GIDEP reporting is to get information about suspect counterfeit parts out as early and as far down the supply chain as possible. However, DOD and industry officials told us they were concerned that GIDEP could not be relied upon to meet this goal if suspect counterfeit parts reports were not made available to industry in a timely and comprehensive manner.

Defense agencies and contractors have varying practices for establishing reasonable certainty after a suspect counterfeit part is discovered. Some DOD officials stated that confirming whether a part is indeed counterfeit requires 1) verification by the manufacturer of that part, 2) completion of a criminal investigation, or 3) comprehensive testing that uncovers multiple strong physical counterfeit indicators. Figure 4 illustrates varying practices for determining whether to submit a GIDEP report.

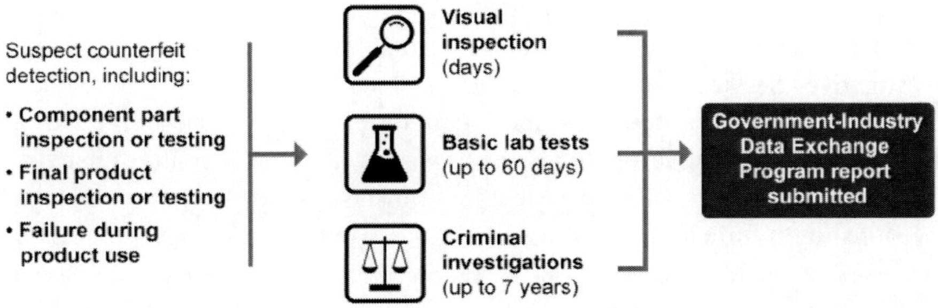


Figure 4. Varying Practices for Government-Industry Data Exchange Program Reporting.

Some defense agencies and contractors have established practices that allow them to meet GIDEP's 60-day reporting requirements. For example, one defense contractor told us it issues a GIDEP report as soon as it has any indication that a part may be counterfeit and another defense contractor told us it conducts routine laboratory tests on any suspect counterfeit parts, which it said can usually be completed within GIDEP's 60-day reporting requirement. The Naval Surface Warfare Center Crane has established a standardized process for evaluating parts suspected of being counterfeit. Specifically, it conducts preliminary engineering investigations to confirm that a part is suspect counterfeit, conducts detailed analysis to calculate scores that measure how certain they are of their suspicions, and then submits GIDEP reports if appropriate. Navy officials explained that they use a scoring system that weights different types of tests and other information differently, depending on their reliability in determining whether a part is counterfeit. The scoring system totals up an overall point-value for an assessment, and officials said they report to GIDEP once the assessment reaches a certain threshold. Navy officials stated that, in general, this process can take from a week to a month, but they can generally meet GIDEP's 60-day reporting requirement.

In contrast, DLA officials said that when DLA first identifies a part as suspect counterfeit, it initially submits a GIDEP report identifying it simply as nonconforming—rather than suspect counterfeit—and with access limited to government use only. It then refers the allegation for a full criminal investigation and, if the investigation confirms that a part is counterfeit, DLA may amend or initiate a new GIDEP report that labels it as counterfeit—however, these investigations can take up to 5 to 7 years. Some defense agency officials said that early GIDEP reporting could interfere with criminal investigations and that reporting needs to wait until indictments are completed so as not to jeopardize the investigation. Officials from the Defense Criminal Investigative Service described certain instances when law enforcement activities may delay releasing suspect counterfeit GIDEP reports, including cases where a covert investigation is underway or there are activities related to a grand jury. However, they noted that these instances are uncommon and that disseminating information takes priority in the event that a suspect counterfeit part poses a health or safety risk. Defense Criminal Investigative Service officials stated that they follow DOD's written procedures for coordination with DOD components.[23]

DLA's practice of not reporting parts to GIDEP as suspect counterfeit until a full investigation has been completed does not align with DLA's policies that require all instances of suspect and confirmed counterfeit parts be documented in GIDEP. According to DLA, 19,000 personnel are trained annually on DLA's counterfeit prevention procedures. However, one DLA official we spoke with acknowledged that although he was trained about the DLA procedures that require them to report any suspect parts, he said that he disagreed with the policy and that GIDEP should only contain confirmed counterfeit parts data.

Some defense contractors are reluctant to allege that a supplier has delivered counterfeit parts without establishing certainty due to concerns about damaging relationships with suppliers up to and including the possibility of being sued if their claims damage the supplier's business. While the 2012 National Defense Authorization Act included language protecting contractors that made a reasonable effort to determine whether a part contained counterfeit or suspect counterfeit parts from civil liability for reporting, contractors we spoke with differed on the extent to which they believe those protections are adequate to protect their financial interests. Some contractors stated that they believe reporting a suspect counterfeit part in GIDEP may leave the contractor open to legal action if the part is determined to be genuine. To address similar concerns, DOD officials said GIDEP established an amnesty period in late

2010 when suspect counterfeit parts reports did not need to include the name of the supplier. Although this temporarily increased reporting, some contractor officials told us that reports without supplier information are difficult to act upon because this information is often necessary for identifying parts in their inventories. As an alternative, contractor officials said it would help alleviate these concerns if GIDEP reporting provided anonymity for the entity submitting the reports, either by having the government submit the report on their behalf or by masking the name of the submitter in the publicly released report.

Air Force and GIDEP officials told us that contractors involved in developing products that will be launched or deployed into space have worked with GIDEP to establish a separate, private system for early reporting of nonconforming parts based on limited information, due to the greater risk associated with incorporating counterfeit or faulty parts in space systems. Some defense officials we spoke with noted that a tiered reporting system—for instance indicating that an early report is based on preliminary information while subsequent updates could be based on a more complete investigation—would increase comfort with reporting suspect counterfeit parts based on limited testing information.

*Standards for Internal Control in the Federal Government* state that management should establish procedures that are effective in accomplishing agency objectives.[24] In the absence of such procedures for determining when to submit suspect counterfeit parts reports in GIDEP, DOD is unable to ensure that the information is submitted in a timely manner, undermining GIDEP's usefulness as an early warning system.

## Industry Is Concerned about Lack of Access to Government Issued GIDEP Reports

Industry was the biggest user of suspect counterfeit part GIDEP reports issued in fiscal years 2011 through 2015, with industry users responsible for 96 percent of all suspect counterfeit GIDEP report downloads. Similarly, as noted previously, 90 percent of the reports were submitted by industry. However, industry officials expressed frustration that access to government-submitted GIDEP reports is often limited to government agencies. As a result, contractors are not able to read them and take responsive actions. We found that most of the suspect counterfeit GIDEP reports submitted by government agencies were not available to industry GIDEP participants. Specifically, 29 of

43 suspect counterfeit GIDEP reports submitted by government agencies in fiscal years 2011 through 2015 were issued with limited access—only viewable by government agencies. In addition, while DOD has other internal information systems that capture information about suspect counterfeit parts, such as PDREP and a department-wide notification system, none of these are fully available to industry participants in the supply chain.

Industry officials told us that, while the quality of GIDEP reports varies, they depend on GIDEP reports because they generally include the most robust information about counterfeit parts among data sources available to them. For instance, industry officials stated that it is very helpful to know the source which supplied a counterfeit part to assess the potential impact of a counterfeit part in the supply chain, but this information is generally not available from other sources. Counterfeit parts GIDEP reports are most useful if they are made available as early as possible, so contractors can take necessary actions before they also purchase the same parts. *Standards for Internal Control in the Federal Government* call for information and communications to be recorded and communicated to others, such as stakeholders who need it, to help the agency achieve its goals.[25] DOD's Counterfeit Prevention Policy does not include guidance about when limiting access to suspect counterfeit parts GIDEP reports is appropriate.

While industry officials told us that individual suspect counterfeit GIDEP reports are useful, they also said it is difficult to analyze GIDEP's data, due to several limitations. For example, they said that the GIDEP information system is more than 15 years old and relies on antiquated technology. In addition, the system is primarily based on downloads of full documents, which limits users' ability to search and analyze reports. According to a senior USD AT&L official, GIDEP staff conduct their own analysis, but do not disseminate all of this information outside their office. GIDEP officials are developing plans to modernize the GIDEP system to accommodate potential access by allies and foreign partners, and address these known limitations. According to the head of GIDEP, several improvements are needed, including updating the website, improving search functions, and improving the capability to extract data for analysis. However, this official stated that no formal decisions have been made as to whether to fund any of these improvements. In addition, a proposed FAR rule, if finalized, would expand the GIDEP reporting requirement to all government agencies' contractors and would require reporting of all nonconforming parts. However, because GIDEP staff reviews each submitted report individually, concerns exist on whether GIDEP staff and technology could handle a large surge in reporting.

# DOD Relies on Contractors to Implement Anti-Counterfeit Systems, but Has Yet to Develop Assessment Guidance

DOD's Counterfeit Prevention Policy depends on coordinated action by both DOD agencies and prime contractors. The DFARS requires prime contractors subject to the cost accounting standards to have anti-counterfeit systems in place; however, the guidance and criteria for DOD to assess these systems are still under development. Consequently, defense contractors have expressed uncertainty about what steps are required of them and which approaches will be deemed adequate by DOD. DOD is working with industry to develop and clarify these standards to avoid and detect counterfeit electronic parts within the defense supply chain. Until the final guidance on how DOD will assess contractors' systems for detecting and avoiding counterfeit electronic parts is in place, DOD will be unable to fully ensure that these anti-counterfeit systems address what is required in the DFARS for counterfeit electronic parts.

## DOD Is Incorporating Counterfeit Parts Policy into Existing Monitoring Activities

DOD's Counterfeit Prevention Policy depends on coordinated action by both DOD agencies and prime contractors. Consequently, the regulations and policies lay out requirements for both public and private entities involved in defense contracting, as well as DOD's responsibilities for overseeing these requirements. Section 818 of the National Defense Authorization Act of 2012 required DOD to implement a program to enhance contractor detection and avoidance of counterfeit electronic parts. Section 818 required the DOD program apply not only to its prime contractors subject to the cost accounting standards, but also to all their subcontractors, regardless of whether the subcontractors were subject to the cost accounting standards. DOD relies heavily on contractors to prevent the introduction of counterfeit materiel into the DOD supply chain, and oversight of these contractor programs to detect and avoid counterfeit electronic parts was delegated to the DCMA. Additionally, Section 818 deems the costs of counterfeit electronic parts and suspect counterfeit electronic parts, including any rework or corrective action required to remedy their use, unallowable, providing incentives for contractors to ensure that they detect counterfeit and suspect counterfeit electronic parts.

When delegated by the contracting officer, DCMA quality assurance and contracting staff oversee a prime contractor's purchasing systems, which can include reviews of the contractor's counterfeit electronic part detection and avoidance system. During these reviews, DCMA staff examine 12 categories of prime contractor compliance—such as reporting and quarantining suspect counterfeit and counterfeit electronic parts— and ensure that they have effective counterfeit detection and avoidance systems. DCMA's initial efforts to assess the status of contractors' counterfeit detection and avoidance systems have begun to identify areas that might require increased oversight. For example, DCMA data as of fall 2015 indicate that approximately 80 percent of suppliers it reviews have processes in place for maintaining part traceability and that approximately 70 percent have processes in place for reporting and quarantining counterfeit or suspect counterfeit electronic parts. DCMA continues to incorporate compliance with counterfeit detection and avoidance in its contractor purchasing system review instruction, but has not yet reviewed any individual contracts for compliance with the r counterfeit electronic parts requirement since it was imposed in 2014.

## Selected Contractors Worked with DOD to Implement Anti-Counterfeit Systems, but DOD Assessment Criteria Is Lacking

Based on our discussions with selected contractors, we found that each of the seven contractors has systems in place to detect and avoid counterfeit parts. These included actions such as: screening of GIDEP and other data sources to identify potential threats of counterfeit parts, using risk analyses to assess the appropriate level of scrutiny for a part, and narrowing the list of suppliers being treated as authorized sources of parts. For at least three of the selected contractors, these business processes predated the DFARS requirement that they have such processes. However, all seven contractors have provided some degree of input to DOD on changes to the laws or additional clarity in guidance that they would like to see.

Collaboration between DOD and industry on proposed rules and policies for the detection and avoidance of counterfeit parts has played an important role in ensuring effective action on both sides. DOD has hosted numerous meetings and interactions between government and industry over the last four years concerning the 2012 National Defense Authorization Act language on counterfeit electronic parts and the development of rules and regulations surrounding it. These have included public meetings by DOD to obtain views on the rulemaking, briefings with DCMA on the adequacy of plans for the detection and avoidance of counterfeit parts, and counterfeit parts enforcement forums with Departments of Justice and Homeland Security. DOD officials stated that these meetings are valuable for crafting DOD policy and setting industry expectations. The contractors we spoke with had all participated in these interactions in some capacity, either directly or through an industry organization, and often both. Some contractors provided both positive and negative views on DOD's engagement, but their responses generally suggest that DOD was listening to the industry, and responding as appropriate.[26]

Despite contractors' efforts to work with DOD in developing and commenting on the rules and regulations, several have expressed concern on the lack of clear criteria on elements such as traceability and testing. They generally indicated that the lack of clear assessment criteria from DCMA on what steps prime contractors should take to meet the requirements in each of the 12 categories complicated their efforts to ensure that their counterfeit detection and avoidance systems meet DFARS requirements. For example, one contractor stated that it would like to use third-party testing of certain electronic parts, but without clear guidance from DCMA on whether this activity would meet certain counterfeit avoidance requirements and which test facilities may be approved for use, it is harder to invest in appropriate solutions. The DFARS states that DOD is to review the acceptability of contractors' counterfeit electronic part detection and avoidance systems.[27] However, according to DCMA officials, DCMA's current guidance is intended to provide flexibility for prime contractors on how they can address each of the 12 categories on which they will be assessed, rather than identify specific procedures.

During our review, DCMA indicated that it is revising its January 2014 instruction on contractor purchasing system reviews to include criteria for assessing counterfeit detection and avoidance systems. In addition, DCMA is updating its counterfeit mitigation instruction to address counterfeit detection and mitigation for DCMA analysts to use while conducting their reviews. *Standards for Internal Control in the Federal Government* state that for an entity to run and control its operations, it must have relevant, reliable, and timely communications relating to internal as well as external events.[28] Both the instruction and the guidebook are intended to assist the DCMA workforce to adequately assess contractor performance to the requirements, but do not provide clarification for industry.

In contrast to DCMA, clarification for industry on how to effectively meet the DFARS criteria has been developed elsewhere in DOD to support counterfeit detection and avoidance in high risk programs. Specifically, MDA provides a checklist to its contractors that goes into greater detail and provides clarity on what MDA will assess as an adequate counterfeit detection and avoidance system. For example, DCMA's checklist generally asks about the flow down of counterfeit avoidance and detection requirements to subcontractors, while MDA's checklist provides the specific steps required to verify flow down. Figure 5 contrasts DCMA and MDA's worksheets for evaluating contractors' counterfeit avoidance and detection systems. Without more detailed clarification on how to meet DCMA criteria, such as that presented in the MDA checklist, contractors cannot be certain how to implement systems that will pass DCMA review.

**Defense Contract Management Agency checklist**

| Does the Contractor's counterfeit part detection and avoidance system include risk-based policies and procedures that address, at a minimum, the following: | | | |
|---|---|---|---|
| EXAMPLE 1. The training of personnel. | Y | INTERNAL INST / POLICIES as noted | There is no evidence that the contractor/supplier(s) processes are implemented. |
| 7. Methodologies to identify suspect counterfeit parts and to rapidly determine if a suspect counterfeit part is, in fact, counterfeit? | | | |
| 8. Design, operation, and maintenance of systems to detect and avoid counterfeit and suspect counterfeit parts? | | | |
| 9 . Flow down of counterfeit avoidance and detection requirements? | | | |

**Missile Defense Agency checklist**

| | | | | | Rating Guidance (0 to 5) | | | | | |
|---|---|---|---|---|---|---|---|---|---|---|
| | Subcontractor Flow Down Verification | | | 0% | 0 | 1 | 2 | Ratings 3 and 4 are removed | 5 | Guidance |
| 11 | Does the contractor maintain a subcontractor compliance assessment schedule for all suppliers of mission and safety critical hardware? | 10 | | 0.0 | No assessment schedule is maintained. | A schedule is maintained, but there are no firm dates, or assessment dates are not being met. | A schedule is maintained, and there are firm dates. Contractor is behind schedule. | | A schedule is maintained per process, and there are firm dates. Contractor is on schedule. Corrective actions are being closed promptly. Assessment summaries are readily available and used to improve the process. | Contractor should have an MDA-approved subcontractor assessment schedule for ensuring flow down of anti-counterfeit requirements to lower tiers. Progress of assessments, including percent completion, should be readily providable. |
| 12 | Does the contractor have documented criteria for defining suppliers of mission and safety critical hardware? | 8 | | 0.0 | No criteria for defining critical suppliers. | | There are general undocumented criteria for identifying critical suppliers. | | There are defined criteria for identifying mission and safety critical suppliers. | For Award Fee compliance, contractor should have an MDA-approved subcontractor assessment schedule for meeting this question. Provide progress of assessments. |
| 13 | How well does the contractor flow the supplier approval items in Section B to the critical subcontractors? | 3 | | 0.0 | None of the supplier selection requirements are flowed down. | The subcontractor must maintain an Approved Supplier Listing and nothing else. | At least three of the Section B questions are flowed as requirements, but customer notification is not one of them. | | All of the Section B questions are flowed as requirements. | Section 3.6.7.1 of the MDA PMAP details the requirements. |

Source: GAO excerpt of defense agency documents. | GAO-16-236.

Figure 5. Comparison of Defense Contract Management Agency and Missile Defense Agency Contractor Evaluations for Counterfeit Detection and Avoidance Systems.

## Contractors Provided Different Perspectives on Applicability and Coverage of Counterfeit Part Regulations

Each of the seven selected contractors we met with told us, and we confirmed through selected contract review, that it was required to flow down—or ensure its subcontractors' contracts included—the DFARS clause requiring subcontractors to have systems to detect and avoid counterfeit electronic parts. These contractors each explained their policies or processes for flowing down these requirements and told us that they use a risk-based approach to oversee subcontractors, including those at lower tiers. These risk-based approaches varied from one contractor to another, but generally involved a preference for purchasing from original part manufacturers or other reliable suppliers, for instance those authorized by the original part manufacturers, and applying greater scrutiny to parts purchased from other sources, and expecting or requiring their subcontractors to do the same.

However, we found disparity on the interpretation of this DFARS clause flowing counterfeit electronic parts regulations down to subcontractors. Specifically, although three of the contractors we spoke with identified no difficulties in effectively passing down these requirements to their subcontractors, four others discussed varying degrees of resistance by their subcontractors, who believed that the DFARS clause did not apply to them. One of these contractors was more specific, noting that many of its suppliers believe that the DFARS clause only flows down to subcontractors covered by the cost accounting standards. In follow-up, the contractor stated that the contract language is generally clear about the requirements for suppliers, but that the focus on prime contractors covered by cost accounting standards can be misleading. Another contractor noted that it had experienced few changes implementing these requirements with its subcontractors, but that it believed other prime contractors and DOD program offices have interpreted the flowdown clause to require the prime to personally review the subcontractor's plan for the detection and avoidance of counterfeit electronic parts, independent of DCMA review.

In addition to confusion associated with flowing down the counterfeit electronic parts requirements to subcontractors, the contractors we spoke with raised some concerns about the coverage of the DFARS counterfeit electronic parts clause requirement. In one context, they expressed concern that gaps in the coverage of the counterfeit parts requirements might be increasing the risk of introducing counterfeit electronic parts in the DOD supply chain. Two contractors stated that the risk of counterfeit parts is largely associated with suppliers that are not covered by cost accounting standards, and that although flowing down these requirements from prime contractors addresses some of this risk, many equally risky subcontractors are suppliers to prime contractors that are not covered by cost accounting standards and therefore are not subject to the DFARS clause or its requirement to flow it down to subcontractors.

However, some contractors noted that commercial suppliers, who the prime contractors consider low-risk, may refrain from working with the government because of these requirements. These contractors told us that the DFARS requirements increase the difficulty of working with commercial suppliers, for whom government contracts represent a small percentage of their overall revenue. They further stated that the costs and burdens of implementing DOD's Counterfeit Prevention Policy, particularly for commercial-off-the-shelf items, outweigh the potential sales to government.

## DOD Counterfeit Detection Efforts Include Improving Testing and Traceability, Collaborating with Other Agencies, and Improving Purchasing Processes

In addition to reporting to GIDEP, DOD and the defense industry have adopted and are developing additional methods to detect and avoid counterfeit parts from entering the DOD supply chain systems. They are working to improve testing to detect counterfeit parts, implementing tools to improve the traceability of electronic parts, sharing information with other government agencies, and improving purchasing processes. These counterfeit detection efforts are critical when the option to procure parts from an authorized source is not available. DOD policies and regulations, and international standards, document the importance of detection efforts, such as testing and authenticating parts, but emphasize that purchasing parts directly from an original component manufacturer or authorized supplier, whenever possible, is the best strategy to avoid counterfeit parts. According to a few officials from the defense industry and DOD, despite the challenges in adopting effective practices and methods to detect counterfeit parts in the U.S. defense supply chain, they are ahead of other countries and international companies in addressing this issue.

### Industry and Government Are Making Improvements to Counterfeit Testing

Industry and government are working collaboratively, as part of an international committee to develop uniform standards for testing counterfeit electronic parts. In 2010, SAE International, an organization that develops international standards for the aerospace and automotive industry, established a subcommittee to develop uniform test method standards for detecting counterfeit electrical, electronic, and electromechanical (electronic) parts. This subcommittee is part of the broader SAE International G-19 committee that previously issued broader standards addressing the risk of counterfeit parts. Representatives of the committee include officials from DOD agencies such as DLA and the Navy, defense contractors, test labs, industry groups, and academia.

According to SAE International, its testing standard will include guidance for determining a part's counterfeit risk, as well as separate documents initially addressing a combination of ten specific test methods for various types of electronic parts counterfeiting. The types of tests include external visual inspection, radiological inspection, x-ray fluorescence, and electrical testing. Once the guidance is issued, it is intended to be applied across the supply chain to include independent testing facilities, distributors and original equipment manufacturers with in-house testing capabilities, and other prime contractors or high-level subcontractors that can flow down the test requirements to their subcontractors. The committee plans to finalize the standard in 2016.

The defense industry has also led efforts to evaluate and improve the quality of testing of suspect counterfeit parts performed by industry, government, and university labs. To address industry and government concerns about testing quality, one prime contractor developed a series of "round robin" tests for labs to compare and assess the quality of their testing with other labs. For the assessment, the contractor sent samples of defective parts to both the contractor's internal testing facilities and independent labs where it outsources testing to determine their accuracy in identifying counterfeit parts. After the test results are compiled, participants receive their results along with other participants' results for comparison, though the names of the other participants are kept confidential. The testing program has expanded to include commercial test labs, contractor in-house labs, distributor in-house labs, government labs, and university labs. The results of these evaluations of testing facilities have been presented to the G-19 committee to inform the development of its test methods standard for counterfeit parts. In addition, NASA officials said that their labs have participated in the round robin testing as part of their efforts to maximize their in-house counterfeit testing capabilities, due to a lack of confidence in external test labs.

## DOD Maintains Internal Testing Capabilities to Detect Evolving Threat of Counterfeit Parts

To support DOD's counterfeit detection efforts, DLA has internal testing capabilities to detect counterfeit parts purchased across the DOD. DLA is responsible for purchasing replacement and support parts for the services, including providing over 90 percent of the military's repair parts, and views that its counterfeit prevention efforts have a critical role in preventing counterfeit parts from entering DOD systems during operations and support phase of a system. To test these parts for quality issues and non-conformances, including testing for suspect counterfeit parts; DLA has product test centers at two locations to conduct three types of tests: mechanical; electronic; and analytical and chemical. DLA's test centers conducts about 13,000 tests a year and have completed over 58,000 total tests from fiscal years 2011 through March 2015, of which 8,925 were specifically for electronic parts. DLA test results do not specifically categorize negative test results as suspect counterfeit, but according to DLA officials, test results may be used for further investigation, which could result in a GIDEP report or a legal action against the supplier. DLA parts testing can be initiated for multiple reasons such as responding to a field complaint or identified discrepancy, random stock sampling, targeted testing of specific vendors with no historical data or past poor performance, or testing of new vendors. DLA officials noted that the test centers have adopted new methods to address evidence of counterfeit parts. For example, a DLA electronic test center created a visual inspection checklist in December 2013 for testing microcircuits to identify defects that could indicate that the part had been previously used or marked, indicating tampering.

The Naval Surface Warfare Center in Crane, Indiana is another facility leading efforts to mitigate the risk of counterfeit parts. It has been providing testing and other support for preventing counterfeit parts from entering Navy systems since 2009. Naval Surface Warfare Center Crane can perform at least 24 types of electrical and physical tests to authenticate and analyze parts to detect counterfeits and has conducted investigations on over 3,000 parts. Naval Surface Warfare Center Crane works with DOD investigative agencies, the intelligence community, and suppliers to acquire and analyze newly discovered forms of counterfeiting in order to adapt new techniques. For example, Naval Surface Warfare Center officials cited an emerging threat whereby clones—exact copies of electronic parts not supplied by the original equipment manufacturer—are being reverse-engineered from stolen intellectual property. In addition to testing parts and working to identify emerging counterfeit threats, Naval Surface Warfare Center Crane, in partnership with MDA, has performed audits and assessments of over 50 independent distributors to evaluate their capabilities to detect counterfeit parts. Figure 6 shows examples of tests to detect suspect counterfeit electronic parts. In response to a provision in the 2016 National Defense Authorization Act, DOD officials noted that Naval Surface Warfare Center Crane is also conducting an assessment of the extent to which counterfeit parts are causing field have caused failures in fielded systems. This assessment is expected to be completed in 2017.[29]

Source: Naval Surface Warfare Center Crane Division. | GAO-16-236

An acoustic microscopy test identified that the center of the part contained a different material that was otherwise undetectable upon visual inspection.

Visual inspection and X-ray revealed part leads that were replaced and covered up.

Figure 6. Examples of Tests to Detect Suspect Counterfeit Electronic Parts.

## DOD Is Improving Parts' Traceability

To minimize the risk of counterfeit parts entering its supply chain, DOD is implementing steps to improve its ability to trace electronic parts back to the original manufacturer and lower supply chain levels. DLA officials told us, for example, that they validate the traceability of 100 percent of their contract awards for microcircuits by applying a botanically-derived marking to all electronic microcircuits—determined to be at a high-risk for counterfeiting—that are purchased by the agency. The marking contains tracking information about the part such as the supplier, lot number, and other identification codes, which can all be retrieved with a hand scanner at any point throughout its serviceable life. DLA places the markings on the surface of the microcircuits at a single facility once it is inspected and its trace documentations authenticating its origin with the original component manufacturer are confirmed. According to DLA officials, DLA applies the marking to about 85,000 microcircuits a year, and is exploring the possibility of expanding the program to other parts that are at high-risk for counterfeiting.

The Defense Advanced Research Projects Agency is also developing a system to authenticate and track electronic parts throughout the supply chain. The Supply Chain Hardware Integrity for Electronics Defense program is developing a microscopic computer chip, which unlike DLA's marking program, will be inserted at the original source of the part and, according to contractor officials, would further strengthen authentication. The microchip will contain a unique identifier for authentication and will record the reliability of the part through the chip's sensors and communications systems. DOD announced that the Defense Advanced Research Projects Agency awarded a development contract for the program in January 2015 and plans to transition the technology to field trials within 3 years, then to industry partners in 4 years once trials are completed. One industry official noted, however, that the success of this program depends upon the willingness of original component manufacturers to implement it.

## DOD Is Collaborating with Federal Agencies to Detect Counterfeit Parts

A group of federal agencies, including DOD, are working collaboratively to improve the detection and interception of counterfeit parts in the defense supply chain. Specifically, Immigration and Customs Enforcement's Homeland Security Investigations within the Department of Homeland Security began an initiative in 2011, called Operation Chain Reaction. This initiative is led by the Department of Homeland Security's National Intellectual Property Rights Coordination Center with a mission to align federal efforts to combat the proliferation of counterfeit goods into the DOD and federal government supply chains. Sixteen federal agencies, including the Defense Criminal Investigative Service, the military investigative services, and the DLA Office of the Inspector General, as well as the Department of Energy, the NASA Office of the Inspector General, and the U.S Customs and Border

Protection are participating in the initiative. Operation Chain Reaction's partnership has had several actions that resulted in detections and seizures of counterfeit parts, including one that resulted in the October 2015 sentencing of a man who imported thousands of counterfeit integrated circuits from China and Hong Kong to resell them to U.S. customers, including contractors supplying them to the U.S. Navy for use in nuclear submarines.

Moreover, in fiscal year 2015, Operation Chain Reaction initiated a pilot program with DLA to validate its current counterfeits prevention practices. By sharing information about DLA inventory with the original manufacturers, this program helps to identify counterfeits in DLA's current supply and evaluate newly ordered parts for authenticity.

## DOD Is Modifying Its Purchasing Processes to Mitigate Counterfeit Risk

As the largest purchaser of electronic parts in DOD, DLA has developed two supplier lists for circumstances in which a part may not be available from an authorized source. In 2009, DLA responded to the risk of counterfeit electronic parts by developing the Qualified Suppliers List of Distributors for companies that sell semiconductors and microcircuits. To be listed, suppliers must meet DLA standards for traceability to the original component manufacturer and part reliability. For instances in which a DLA buyer cannot source a supplier with appropriate authentication credentials or traceability no longer exists, DLA created the Qualified Testing Suppliers List of semiconductor and microcircuit suppliers in 2012 that meet DLA-approved testing and other quality assurance standards for the parts. All listed suppliers must meet criteria established by DLA and be subject to onsite audits. Once approved for either program, participants can be subject to random site audits, and are audited on a regular basis. According to DLA officials, these audits can occur every 2 to 5 years, based on the perceived risk of the supplier. These lists have 39 and 20 suppliers respectively. A senior DLA official noted that the development of these lists has allowed DLA to limit its supplier base to certain suppliers but still provide enough suppliers for sufficient competition. The official added that if DLA cannot procure these types of parts from an original component manufacturer, authorized manufacturer, or listed supplier and has to use another distributor, then the part will be subject to product verification testing.

In addition, DLA, the Navy, and the Office of the Secretary of Defense are upgrading the Past Performance Information Retrieval System, which serves as a government-wide repository of contractor past performance data, to include counterfeit parts and supplier data in order to identify procurement risk. As part of the system's planned capabilities, it will serve as a repository for contractor and item risk assessments based on information from multiple sources including PDREP, GIDEP, product testing, and contractor suspension and debarment history. According to DLA and Navy officials we spoke with, this program, once implemented, will incorporate all the data for analyses and predict probabilities for the chance of a supplier to introduce counterfeit materials into the supply chain. The first phase of the enhancements has already been completed to allow users to identify suppliers that have been excluded or debarred for reasons, such as selling counterfeit parts, and allows agencies to flag certain high-risk parts that have been counterfeited in the past. The program is expected to be completed by early fiscal year 2018, according to a Navy official. Initially, DOD will have sole access to the new system, but according to DOD officials, future planned enhancements may include providing access to other federal agencies.

## CONCLUSION

The DOD supply chain is vulnerable to the risk of counterfeit parts—which can have serious consequences. To effectively identify and mitigate this risk, DOD and its defense contractors need data on the existence of counterfeit parts in their supply chain; whether those be suspected or confirmed counterfeit. Three years after GIDEP reporting became mandatory, we found evidence that this system may not be effective as an early warning system to prevent counterfeit parts from entering the supply chain. Without proper oversight to ensure the reporting requirement is consistently applied, DOD cannot depend on GIDEP data to ensure it is effectively managing the risks associated with counterfeit parts. DOD's lack of insight into DLA's reporting practices is particularly problematic, given DLA's key role in procuring parts for the department. Further, without a standardized process for establishing the level of evidence needed to submit suspect counterfeit GIDEP reports, defense agencies—particularly DLA—and contractors have demonstrated a reluctance to report suspect parts, creating a delay in knowledge-sharing and an opportunity for counterfeit parts to be used in defense products. Also, DOD needs to be sure that information in GIDEP about suspect counterfeit parts is reaching industry participants whenever possible, but currently lacks necessary guidance to ensure this occurs.

In addition, DOD relies on its prime contractors and subcontractors to have systems in place to detect and avoid counterfeit parts, but DOD has not yet clarified for industry the criteria by which it will assess and monitor those systems. Without providing further clarification about the criteria against which they will be evaluated, DOD cannot effectively empower its prime contractors and subcontractors to perform their critical role in consistently protecting the supply chain from counterfeit parts. Moreover, recent efforts by DOD and the defense industry to improve part traceability and testing are taking shape, but these efforts cannot be appropriately targeted to the greatest risk vulnerabilities without complete data on the existence of counterfeit parts.

## RECOMMENDATIONS FOR EXECUTIVE ACTION

To provide greater compliance with the GIDEP reporting requirement among the DOD components and their defense supplier-base, we recommend that the Undersecretary of Defense for Acquisition, Technology and Logistics take the following three steps:

- Establish mechanisms for department-wide oversight of defense agencies' compliance with the GIDEP reporting requirement.
- Develop a standardized process for determining the level of evidence needed to report a part as suspect counterfeit in GIDEP, such as a tiered reporting structure in GIDEP that provides an indication of where the suspect part is in the process of being assessed.
- Develop guidance for when access to GIDEP reports should be limited to only government users or made available to industry.

To help DOD and contractors to have a greater degree of certainty and consistency to adhere to the requirements for contractor counterfeit detection and avoidance systems, we recommend that the Undersecretary of Defense for Acquisition, Technology and Logistics:

- Clarify for industry the criteria by which DOD will assess contractor counterfeit detection and avoidance systems.

## AGENCY COMMENTS AND OUR EVALUATION

We provided a draft copy of this report to the Departments of Defense, Energy, Homeland Security, Justice, and Transportation; as well as the Administrator of the National Aeronautics and Space Administration for their comment. In written comments, DOD concurred with our three recommendations directed at providing greater compliance with the GIDEP reporting requirement among the DOD components and their defense supplier-base. Specifically, DOD plans to issue a new Instruction on GIDEP in fiscal year 2017, covering the identification of roles and responsibilities for submitting GIDEP reports and oversight; the level of evidence needed to report a part as suspect counterfeit in GIDEP; and the use of GIDEP, including guidance for when access to GIDEP reports should be restricted to government only. DOD partially concurred with our recommendation aimed at helping DOD and its contractors to have a greater degree of certainty and consistency to adhere to the requirements for contractor counterfeit detection and avoidance systems. Specifically, DOD stated that it agrees with informing contractors on how their counterfeit detection and avoidance systems will be assessed; however, it does not agree with prescribing specific counterfeit detection and avoidance system implementation details. We continue to believe it is important that DOD strengthen its communication with the contractors and as our recommendation indicated, for DOD to clarify the criteria by which it will assess contractor's counterfeit detection and avoidance systems —which is different than providing specific implementation details. *Standards for Internal Control in the Federal Government* state that for an entity to run and control its operations, it must have relevant, reliable and timely communication related to internal and external events, which includes providing relevant and reliable criteria to contractors so that they can appropriately develop or improve their systems to detect and avoid counterfeit parts in order for them to be determined sufficient by DOD. Providing these criteria allows contractors greater visibility into DOD's expectations. DOD also provided technical comments, which we incorporated as appropriate.

The Departments of Energy, Homeland Security, and the National Aeronautics and Space Administration provided technical comments, which we incorporated as appropriate. The Departments of Justice and Transportation did not provide comments for this review.

Marie A. Mak
Director, Acquisition and Sourcing Management

# APPENDIX I: OBJECTIVES, SCOPE, AND METHODOLOGY

The report focuses on reporting of counterfeit parts and the detection and avoidance of counterfeit parts in the Department of Defense (DOD) supply chain. Specifically, our objectives were to determine (1) the use of the Government-Industry Data Exchange Program (GIDEP) to report suspect counterfeit parts, from fiscal years 2011 through 2015; (2) the effectiveness of GIDEP reporting as an early warning system for counterfeit parts; (3) the extent to which DOD has assessed defense contractors' systems for detecting and avoiding counterfeit parts; and (4) key ongoing efforts by selected government and industry organizations to improve the detection and reporting of counterfeit or suspect counterfeit parts.

We met with DOD officials and reviewed counterfeit mitigation policies and procedures from the Office of the Under Secretary of Defense for Acquisition, Technology, and Logistics (USD AT&L) Logistic and Materiel Readiness, Supply Chain Integration and USD AT&L Defense Procurement and Acquisition Policy, as well as the military services and other DOD components including the Departments of the Army, Navy, and Air Force, the Missile Defense Agency (MDA), Defense Logistics Agency (DLA), Defense Contract Management Agency (DCMA), and the Defense Criminal Investigative Service. We then assessed DOD's policies, procedures and practices against criteria in *Standards for Internal Control in the Federal Government*.[1]

To determine use of GIDEP to report suspect counterfeit parts over the last 5 fiscal years, we obtained the complete GIDEP database for reports entered between October 1, 2010 and September 30, 2015. We analyzed the data to identify GIDEP reports that were categorized as suspect counterfeit and determine trends in reporting by fiscal year and across entities who submitted the reports. We assessed GIDEP by reviewing documentation and meeting with GIDEP officials, and determined that the data were sufficiently reliable for our purposes. To understand the trends in GIDEP reporting, we interviewed Air Force, Army, DCMA, DLA, MDA, and Navy officials as well as representatives from selected defense contractors and industry associations.

To assess the effectiveness of GIDEP reporting as an early warning system for counterfeit parts, we interviewed Air Force, Army, USD AT&L, DCMA, DLA, MDA, and Navy officials as well as representatives from selected defense contractors and industry associations. In addition, we analyzed data in DOD's Product Data Reporting and Evaluation Program (PDREP) submitted between October 2010 and August 2015, the most complete data available when we conducted this analysis, to identify product quality reports coded as suspect counterfeit and assess the extent to which these reports overlapped with GIDEP suspect counterfeit reports. We assessed the PDREP data by reviewing documentation and meeting with PDREP officials, and determined that the data were sufficiently reliable for our purposes. Further, we met with officials from the Defense Criminal Investigative Service and the Department of Justice to discuss how ongoing criminal cases may impact timely GIDEP reporting.

To assess the extent to which DOD has assessed defense contractors' systems for detecting and avoiding counterfeit parts, we reviewed Section 818 of the 2012 National Defense Authorization Act, the Federal Acquisition Regulation (FAR), and the Defense Federal Acquisition Regulation Supplement (DFARS) related to detecting, reporting, and mitigating counterfeit electronic parts in the DOD supply chain by defense contractors.[2] We reviewed documents and spoke with officials at DCMA regarding DCMA's process and criteria for determining the sufficiency of contractors' systems to detect and avoid counterfeit electronic parts. We interviewed seven major defense contractors with awards containing DFARS counterfeit electronic parts language to discuss and examine their policies to detect and avoid counterfeit parts—BAE Systems, Boeing, General Dynamics, Lockheed Martin, Northrop Grumman, Raytheon, and Sikorsky Aircraft. To select these contractors, we obtained data from Defense Procurement Acquisition Policy identifying all 2014 DOD awards and contract actions containing the DFARS counterfeit electronic parts language and selected the five contractors with the largest dollar value of such actions, as well as two other contractors with smaller, but still significant, total volume. Additionally, for each of these contractors, we non-judgmentally selected one contract from the 2014 dataset, covering a range of award values and products and services, to examine how DOD counterfeit parts requirements for contractors are applied in a variety of situations. In addition, we met with industry associations representing companies from various levels of the defense industry supply chain, including the Aerospace Industry Association, Semiconductor Industry Association, and the Independent Distributors of Electronics Association to determine how and to what extent they worked with DOD to implement to federal regulations for counterfeit mitigation and the impact of regulations related to the detection and avoidance of counterfeit electronic parts.

To identify key ongoing efforts by selected government and industry organizations to improve the detection and reporting of counterfeit or suspect counterfeit parts, we reviewed documents and data and contacted officials from Defense agencies, including Defense Advanced Research Products Agency, DLA Headquarters, and DLA Land and Maritime, as well as other government agencies, such as the National Aeronautics and Space Administration, the Department of Energy, Department of Homeland Security, and the Department of Transportation. We also obtained documents and met with representatives from SAE International and the G-19 Counterfeit Electronic Parts Committee to gain an understanding of the standards and practices being developed to detect and avoid counterfeit parts. We also met with selected defense contractors to discuss actions taken to improve their practices to detect and avoid counterfeit parts, as well as reviewed data and interviewed a representative from ERAI, related to the reporting of potential counterfeit parts. In addition, we visited the product testing facilities at DLA Land and Maritime in Columbus, Ohio and the Naval Surface Warfare Center in Crane, Indiana. In addition, we met with representatives from the Center for Advanced Life Cycle Engineering and attended a symposium about counterfeit parts and materials organized by the Center for Advanced Life Cycle Engineering and the Surface Mount Technology Association in College Park, MD.

We conducted this performance audit from January 2015 to February 2016 in accordance with generally accepted government auditing standards. Those standards require that we plan and perform the audit to obtain sufficient, appropriate evidence to provide a reasonable basis for our findings and conclusions based on our audit objectives. We believe that the evidence obtained provides a reasonable basis for our findings and conclusions based on our audit objectives.

# APPENDIX II: NUMBER OF GOVERNMENT-INDUSTRY DATA EXCHANGE PROGRAM (GIDEP) REPORTS BY ROLE IN SUPPLY CHAIN OF ENTITY SUBMITTING REPORT (FISCAL YEARS 2011-2015)

| Report Submitter Type | 2011 | 2012 | 2013 | 2014 | 2015 | Total Reports |
|---|---|---|---|---|---|---|
| Contractor Category | | | | | | |
| Test Lab | 72 | 0 | 0 | 0 | 0 | 72 |
| Original EquipmentManufacturers | 27 | 76 | 26 | 25 | 24 | 178 |
| Authorized Distributors | 2 | 0 | 0 | 1 | 0 | 3 |
| Independent Distributors | 152 | 15 | 16 | 10 | 14 | 207 |

**(Continued)**

| Report Submitter Type | 2011 | 2012 | 2013 | 2014 | 2015 | Total Reports |
|---|---|---|---|---|---|---|
| Midlevel Manufacturers | 6 | 7 | 3 | 5 | 0 | 21 |
| Original Component Manufacturers | 0 | 2 | 0 | 0 | 0 | 2 |
| Contractor subtotal | 259 | 100 | 45 | 41 | 38 | 483 |
| Government Agency | | | | | | |
| Defense: Navy | 1a | 19 | 0 | 1 | 3 | 24 |
| Defense: DLA | 0 | 5 | 3 | 0 | 1 | 9 |
| Defense: DCMA | 1 | 1 | 1 | 1 | 0 | 4 |
| Defense: Defense Microelectronics Agency | 0 | 1 | 1 | 1 | 0 | 3 |
| Department of Energy | 0 | 0 | 2 | 0 | 1 | 3 |
| Government Subtotal | 2 | 26 | 7 | 3 | 5 | 43 |
| Total | 261 | 126 | 52 | 44 | 43 | 526 |

Source: GAO analysis of GIDEP data and classifications of reporting entities. | GAO-16-236

Note: The GIDEP database does not have information about the roles in the supply chain of entities submitting reports. Categorization of these entities was completed by GIDEP staff based on their expertise and could not be independently verified by GAO.

[a]The Navy's GIDEP operations center entered a report in 2011 on behalf of the Consumer Product Safety Commission.

## End Notes

[1] S. Rep. No. 113-176, at 148 (2011).

[2] GAO, *Standards for Internal Control in the Federal Government*, GAO/AIMD-00-21.3.1 (Washington, D.C.: Nov. 1999).

[3] SAE International, AS6174A, Counterfeit Materiel; Assuring Acquisition of Authentic and Conforming Materiel, Revised July 2014 and AS6081, Fraudulent/Counterfeit Electronic Parts: Avoidance, Detection, Mitigation, and Disposition – Distributors, November 2012.

[4] GAO, *Defense Supplier Base: DOD Should Leverage Ongoing Initiatives In Developing Its Program to Mitigate Risk of Counterfeit Parts*, GAO-10-389, (Washington, D.C.: Mar. 29, 2010); GAO, *Space and Missile Acquisitions: Periodic Assessment Needed to Correct Parts Quality Problems in Major Programs*, GAO-11-404, (Washington, D.C.: Jun. 24, 2011); GAO, *DOD Supply Chain: Suspect Counterfeit Electronic Parts Can Be Found on Internet Purchasing Platforms*, GAO-12-375, (Washington, D.C.: Feb. 21, 2012).

[5] S. Rep. 112-167, Inquiry Into Counterfeit Electronic Parts in The Department of Defense Supply Chain (2012).

[6] National Defense Authorization Act for Fiscal Year 2012. Pub. L. No. 112-81 (Dec 31, 2011).

[7] These requirements apply to prime contractors subject to cost accounting standards on acquisitions other than small business set-asides. The cost accounting standards are rules designed to ensure contractors consistently apply cost accounting practices to contracts with the government. These standards are prescribed by the cost accounting standards board under 41 U.S.C. § 1502.

[8] DOD implemented its cost principle that costs are not allowable unless 1) the contractor has an operational system to detect and avoid counterfeit parts that has been approved by DOD 2) the parts are government-furnished property, and 3) the contractor provided notice to the government within 60 days after the contract became aware of the suspected counterfeit part. DFARS § 231.205-71.

[9] Department of Defense Instruction 4140.67 DOD Counterfeit Prevention Counterfeit Prevention Policy, April 26, 2013. "Materiel" refers to military materials and equipment.

[10] PDREP is managed by the Navy and is also used by the Army, DLA and the Defense Contract Management Agency. The Joint Deficiency Reporting System is used by the Air Force and Naval Air Systems Command.

[11] The Office of Federal Procurement Policy's cost accounting standards cover a much broader range of requirements than just anti-counterfeit systems, and generally apply to those contractors receiving at least $50 million in government contracts. DFARS § 246.870-3(b) excludes small business set-aside contracts from the counterfeit prevention requirements, even if the contractor is subject to cost accounting standards.

[12] Under the FAR, contracts must include quality requirements, such as testing, inspection, and surveillance, necessary to protect the government's interest. The contractor is responsible for controlling the quality of its supplies or services while the government is responsible for contract quality assurance. Agencies have wide latitude to adjust quality assurance requirements according to the type of acquisition. The new DFARS counterfeit detection and avoidance policies provide more specific quality requirements. FAR §§ 46.102(a); 46.103(a); 46.105(a); 46.101; 46.401(a).

[13] We did not include failure analysis reports – a particular GIDEP report type that addresses the root cause of part failures or suitability – in our analysis because GIDEP no longer identifies them as counterfeit parts reports for future submissions, in part because they generally do not include the information – such as supplier names – industry and government entities needs to manage the risks of counterfeit parts.

[14] GIDEP does not classify entities by their role in the supply chain. To categorize entities that submitted counterfeit parts reports in GIDEP, we asked GIDEP staff to provide these classifications but we could not independently verify them.

[15] Some GIDEP reports name multiple suppliers.

[16] GAO/AIMD-00-21.3.1.

[17] GAO/AIMD-00-21.3.1.

[18] Debarment is an administrative remedy that agencies may use to protect the government's interests by excluding individuals, contractors, and grantees from receiving federal contracts, grants, and other forms of financial assistance based on various types of misconduct.

[19] We did not include PDREP reports issued in September 2015 in our analysis because we conducted our analysis prior to the end of fiscal year 2015.

[20] We did not assess the reliability of ERAI's data.

[21] GIDEP Operations Manual, Chapter 7. para. 7.3 (2015).

[22] DOD Instruction 4140.67, DOD Counterfeit Prevention Policy, para. 3.d (April 26, 2013).

[23] Defense of Defense Instruction 7050.05, "Corruption of Remedies for Fraud and Corruption Related to Procurement Activities," May 12, 2014.

[24] GAO/AIMD-00-21.3.1.

[25] GAO/AIMD-00-21.3.1.

[26] Because this was a small, non-generalizable sample of prime contractors, these views should not be taken as representative of the defense industry as a whole.

[27] DFARS § 252.246-7007(d).

[28] GAO/AIMD-00-21.3.1.

[29] Section 238, FY16 NDAA, Pub. L. No. 114-92 (Nov 25, 2015).

## End Notes for Appendix I

[1] GAO, *Standards for Internal Control in the Federal Government*, GAO/AIMD-00-21.3.1 (Washington, D.C.: Nov. 1999).

[2] DFARS §§ 231.205-71, 244.303, 244.305-71, 246.870-1, 246.870-2, 246.870-3, 252.244-7001, and 252.246-7007; for proposed FAR amendments, see 79 Federal Register 33164 (June 10, 2014), proposing amendments to FAR §§ 2.101, 7.105, 12.208, 12.301, 46.101, 46.102, 46.105, 46.202-1, 46.317, 46.407, 52.213-4, 52.244-6, and a new clause at 52.246-XX.

In: Counterfeit Parts
Editor: Erik Dawson
ISBN: 978-1-63485-989-9


*Chapter 2*

# DOD SUPPLY CHAIN: SUSPECT COUNTERFEIT ELECTRONIC PARTS CAN BE FOUND ON INTERNET PURCHASING PLATFORMS*

*United States Government Accountability Office*

## ABBREVIATIONS

| | |
|---|---|
| DLA | Defense Logistics Agency |
| DOD | Department of Defense |
| RTS | resistance to solvents |
| SEM | scanning electron microscopy |
| XRF | X-ray florescence |

## WHY GAO DID THIS STUDY

Counterfeit parts—generally the misrepresentation of parts' identity or pedigree—can seriously disrupt the Department of Defense (DOD) supply chain, harm weapon systems integrity, and endanger troops' lives. In a

* This is an edited, reformatted and augmented version of The United States Government Accountability Office publication, GAO-12-375, dated February 2012.

November testimony (GAO-12-213T), GAO summarized preliminary observations from its investigation into the purchase and authenticity testing of selected, military-grade electronic parts that may enter the DOD supply chain. As requested, this report presents GAO's final findings on this issue. The results are based on a nongeneralizable sample and cannot be used to make inferences about the extent to which parts are being counterfeited.

GAO created a fictitious company and gained membership to two Internet platforms providing access to vendors selling military-grade electronic parts. GAO requested quotes from numerous vendors to purchase a total of 16 parts from three categories: (1) authentic part numbers for obsolete and rare parts; (2) authentic part numbers with postproduction date codes (date codes after the last date the part was manufactured); and (3) bogus, or fictitious, part numbers that are not associated with any authentic parts. To determine whether the parts received were counterfeit, GAO contracted with a qualified, independent testing lab for full component authentication analysis of the first two categories of parts, but not the third (bogus) category. Part numbers have been altered for reporting purposes.

GAO is not making recommendations in this report.

## What GAO Found

Suspect counterfeit and bogus—part numbers that are not associated with any authentic parts—military-grade electronic parts can be found on Internet purchasing platforms, as none of the 16 parts vendors provided to GAO were legitimate. "Suspect counterfeit," which applies to the first two categories of parts that were tested, is the strongest term used by an independent testing lab, signifying a potential violation of intellectual property rights, copyrights, or trademark laws, or misrepresentation to defraud or deceive. After submitting requests for quotes on both platforms, GAO received responses from 396 vendors, of which 334 were located in China; 25 in the United States; and 37 in other countries, including the United Kingdom and Japan. Of the 16 parts purchased, vendors usually responded within a day. GAO selected the first of any vendor among those offering the lowest prices that provided enough information to purchase a given part, generally within 2 weeks. Under GAO's selection methodology, all 16 parts were provided by vendors in China.

Specifically, all 12 of the parts received after GAO requested rare part numbers or postproduction date codes were suspect counterfeit, according to the testing lab. Multiple authentication tests, ranging from inspection with electron microscopes to X-ray analysis, revealed that the parts had been remarked to display the part numbers and manufacturer logos of authentic parts. Other features were found to be deficient from military standards, such as the metallic composition of certain pieces. For the parts requested using postproduction date codes, the vendors also altered date markings to represent the parts as newer than when they were last manufactured, as verified by the parts' makers. Finally, after submitting requests for bogus parts using invalid part numbers, GAO purchased four parts from four vendors, which shows their willingness to supply parts that do not technically exist.

* * *

February 21, 2012

The Honorable Carl Levin
Chairman

The Honorable John McCain
Ranking Member
Committee on Armed Services United States Senate

Counterfeit parts—generally the misrepresentation of parts' identity or pedigree—have the potential to seriously disrupt the Department of Defense (DOD) supply chain, delay missions, affect the integrity of weapon systems, and ultimately endanger the lives of our troops. Almost anything is at risk of being counterfeited, from fasteners used on aircraft to electronics used on missile guidance systems. There can be many sources of counterfeit parts as DOD draws from a large network of global suppliers.[1]

In 2011, we reported that the increase in counterfeit electronic parts is one of several potential barriers DOD faces in addressing parts quality problems.[2] More recently, you asked about the availability of counterfeit parts on Internet platforms commonly used to buy hard-to-find military-grade electronic parts, including those used in weapon systems. In a November testimony, we summarized preliminary observations from our investigation into the purchase and authenticity testing of selected, military-grade electronic parts that may enter the DOD supply chain.[3] This report presents our final findings on this issue.

In conducting this investigation, we created a fictitious company to gain access to Internet platforms that provide access to vendors selling military-grade electronic parts. Our company included a fictitious owner and employees, mailing and e-mail addresses, a website, and a listing on the Central Contractor Registration.[4] We attempted to purchase memberships to three Internet platforms that were of interest to this committee. One platform granted us membership despite not receiving all requested supporting documentation, the second granted us membership after we supplied the requested documentation as well as fictitious business references, and the third denied our request for membership even after we provided all documentation and references. None of the platforms contacted our references. We then requested quotes from vendors on both platforms to purchase a total of 16 parts from three categories: (1) authentic part numbers for obsolete and rare parts; (2) authentic part numbers with postproduction date codes (date codes after the last date the part was manufactured); and (3) bogus, or fictitious, part numbers that are not associated with any authentic parts. Using a list of four authentic part numbers this committee provided, we purchased 7 parts from the first category and 5 parts from the second (for which we altered only the date code). We independently verified with the Defense Logistics Agency (DLA) that these part numbers were used for military applications using DLA's Federal Logistics Information System and by interviewing DLA officials.[5] We used three invalid part numbers provided by the committee, which altered portions of existing part numbers that identify certain performance specifications, to purchase the 4 bogus parts. We then confirmed with DLA and selected part manufacturers that the numbers we developed were invalid. We altered all part numbers for reporting purposes.

We requested parts from vendors that were new in original packaging, not refurbished, and had no mixed date codes. We selected the first vendor among those offering the lowest prices that provided enough information, such as name, addresses, and payment method, to make a purchase. We attempted to avoid using the same vendor more than once unless no other vendor responded to our request; however, vendors may operate under more than one name. We did not attempt to verify the independence of any vendor before we made our purchases. Finally, we contracted with the SMT Corp. for full component authentication analysis.[6] For details on this analysis, see appendix I.

The results of this investigation are based on the use of a nongeneralizable sample, and these results cannot be used to make inferences about the extent to which parts are being counterfeited. We conducted this investigation from August 2011 to February 2012 in accordance with standards prescribed by the Council of the Inspectors General on Integrity and Efficiency.

## SUSPECT COUNTERFEIT ELECTRONIC PARTS CAN BE FOUND ON INTERNET PURCHASING PLATFORMS

As shown in figure 1, each of the 16 parts we purchased was either suspect counterfeit or bogus. Specifically, all 12 of the parts we received after requesting authentic part numbers (either with valid or invalid date codes) were suspect counterfeit, according to SMT Corp. In addition, vendors provided us with 4 bogus parts after we requested invalid part numbers, which demonstrates their willingness to sell parts that do not technically exist. The following sections detail our findings for each of the three categories of parts we purchased.

Under our selection methodology, the 16 parts we purchased were provided by 13 vendors in China. After submitting requests for quotes on both platforms, we received responses from 396 vendors, of which 334 were located in China; 25 in the United States; and 37 in other countries, including the United Kingdom and Japan. All 40 of the responses we received for the bogus part numbers were from vendors located in China (6 of these vendors also offered to sell us parts for the authentic part numbers we requested). We selected the first of any vendor among those offering the lowest prices that provided enough information to purchase a given part, generally within 2 weeks.[7] As such, 3 vendors each supplied 2 parts and 10 vendors each supplied 1 part. We sent 13 payments to Shenzhen, 2 payments to Shantou, and 1 payment to Beijing. Despite operating under different company names, 2 vendors provided us with identical information for sending payment (name of representative and contact information). There could be a number of explanations for this, ranging from legitimate (the vendors handle payments through the same banker or accountant) to potentially deceptive (same individuals representing themselves as multiple companies). Thirteen parts were then shipped from Shenzhen and 3 from Hong Kong.

### Category 1: Authentic Part Numbers for Obsolete or Rare Parts

All seven of the obsolete or rare parts that SMT Corp. tested were suspected counterfeits. Each part failed multiple component authentication analyses, including visual, chemical, X-ray, and microscopic testing. The parts were purchased from five different vendors. Figure 2 provides photos and detailed test results for each part.

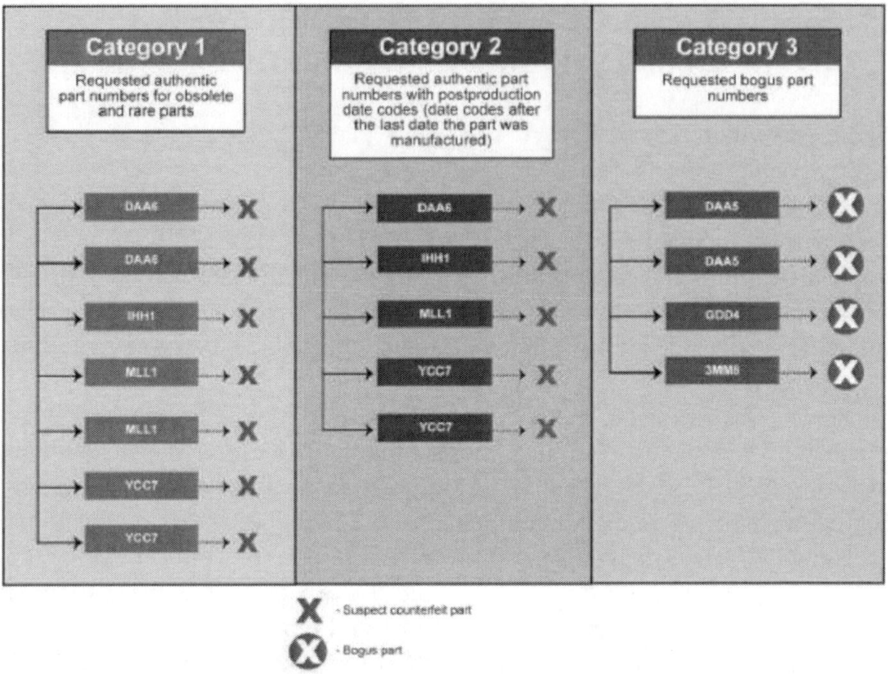


Source: GAO analysis of SMT test results.

Note: Part numbers shown have been altered from the part numbers used for purchasing.

Figure 1. Status of Parts Purchased and Tested.

*DAA6 (two parts purchased).* Both purchases made using part number DAA6 contained samples that failed multiple authentication analyses, leading SMT Corp. to conclude that the parts were suspect counterfeit.

Both parts were purchased from different vendors using the same part number, but were not identical, as shown in figure 2. An authentic part with this part number is an operational amplifier that may be commonly found in the Army and Air Force's Joint Surveillance and Target Attack Radar System; the Air Force's F-15 Eagle fighter plane; and the Air Force, Navy, and Marine Corps's Maverick AGM-65A missile. If authentic, this part converts input voltages into output voltages that can be hundreds to thousands of times larger. Failure can lead to unreliable operation of several components (e.g., integrated circuits) in the system and poses risks to the function of the system where the parts reside.

**Category 1**

Requested authentic part numbers for obsolete and rare parts

| Analysis performed | DAA6 | DAA6 | IHH1 | MLL1 | MLL1 | YCC7 | YCC7 |
|---|---|---|---|---|---|---|---|
| Visual Inspection | Fail | Fail | Fail | Fail | Fail | Fail | Fail |
| Resistance to Solvents (RTS) and Scrape Test | N/A | N/A | Fail | N/A | N/A | Pass | Pass |
| Package Configuration and Dimensions | Pass | Pass | Pass | Pass | Pass | Pass | Fail |
| X-Ray Florescence Elemental Analysis | Fail | Fail | Pass | Fail | Fail | Pass | Pass |
| Real-Time X-ray Analysis | Pass | Fail | Pass | Pass | Pass | Fail | Pass |
| Scanning Electron Microscopy (SEM) Analysis | Fail | Fail | Fail | Pass | Pass | Fail | Fail |
| Solderability Test | Pass | Pass | Pass | Pass | Pass | Pass | Pass |
| Dynasolve Test | N/A | N/A | Fail | N/A | N/A | N/A | Fail |
| Delidding and Die Microscopy | Fail | Fail | Fail | Fail | Fail | Fail | Pass |
| **Suspect counterfeit** | **Yes** | **Yes** | **Yes** | **Yes** | **Yes** | **Yes** | **Yes** |

Source: GAO analysis of SMT test results.

Note: Part numbers shown have been altered from the part numbers used for purchasing. N/A Indicated that the analysis was not performed because the unique properties of the part render the test inapplicable or prevent the test from being performed.

Figure 2. Authentication Analysis Results of Obsolete or Rare Parts.

The part we received from one vendor failed four of seven authentication analyses. Visual inspection found inconsistencies, including different or missing markings and scratches, which suggested that samples were remarked. Scanning electron microscopy (SEM) analysis revealed further evidence of re-marking. X-ray fluorescence (XRF) testing of the samples revealed that the leads contain no lead (Pb) instead of the 3 percent lead (Pb) required by military specifications.[8,9] Five samples were chosen for delidding, which exposes parts' die, because of their side marking inconsistencies. While all five samples had the same die, the die markings were inconsistent.[10] According to SMT Corp., die markings in components manufactured within the same date and lot code should be consistent. Finally, the devices found in the first lot tested went into "last time buy" status in 2001, meaning that the parts were misrepresented as newer than they actually were. The manufacturer confirmed this status and added that the part marking did not match its marking scheme, meaning that the date code marked on the samples would not be possible.

The part received from the second vendor failed five of seven authentication analyses. Visual inspection again found inconsistencies, including additional markings on about half the samples. Further, scratches and reconditioned leads indicated that the parts were removed from a working environment—that is, not new as we requested. SEM analysis corroborated these findings. As with the other DAA6 part, XRF testing revealed that the leads contain no lead (Pb). X-rays revealed different sized die, and delidding revealed that the die were differently marked.

*IHH1 (one part purchased).* The purchase made using part number IHH1 contained samples that failed five of nine authentication analyses, leading SMT Corp. to conclude that the part was suspect counterfeit. An authentic part with this part number is a multiplexer, which allows electronic signals from several different sources to be checked at one location. It has been used in at least 63 different DOD weapon systems, including the Air Force Special Operations Forces' AC-130H Gunship aircraft, the Air Force's B-2B aircraft, and the Navy's E-2C Hawkeye aircraft. If at least one of the specific signals is critical to the successful operation of the system, then failure could pose a risk to the system overall.

Visual inspection revealed numerous issues, including color differences in the top and bottom of the part's surfaces, suggesting resurfacing and re-marking. Large amounts of scuffs and scratches, foreign debris, and substandard leads were also found. The part also failed resistance to solvents (RTS) testing when it resulted in removal of resurfacing material. Further, Dynasolve testing (additional RTS testing) revealed remnants of a completely different manufacturer and part number. SEM showed evidence of lapping, which is the precise removal of a part's material to produce the desired dimensions, finish, or shape. Finally, delidding showed die that were similar but insufficiently marked to determine whether they matched the authentic part number. However, because of the failure of the Dynasolve testing, the die cannot be correct.

*MLL1 (two parts purchased).* Both purchases made using part number MLL1 contained a number of samples that failed three of seven authentication analyses, leading SMT Corp. to conclude that the parts were suspect counterfeit. Both parts were purchased from different vendors using the same part number, but were not identical, as shown in figure 2. An authentic part with this number is a voltage regulator that may be commonly found in military systems such as the Air Force's KC-130 Hercules aircraft, the Navy's F/A-18E Super Hornet fighter plane, the Marine Corps's V-22 Osprey aircraft, and the Navy's SSN-688 Los Angeles Class nuclear-powered attack submarine. If authentic, these parts provide accurate power voltage to segments of the system they serve. Failure can lead to unreliable operation of several components (e.g., integrated circuits) in the system and poses risks to the function of the system where the parts reside.

The parts received from both vendors failed the same authentication analyses. Visual inspection was performed on all evidence samples from both purchases. Different color epoxy seals were noted within both lots, according to SMT Corp., which is common in suspect counterfeit devices because many date and lot codes are re-marked to create a uniform appearance. Moreover, XRF testing of the samples revealed that the leads contain no lead (Pb); according to military performance standards, leads should be alloyed with at least 3 percent of lead (Pb).[11] Further, XRF data between the top and bottom of the lead revealed inconsistencies in chemical composition, leading SMT Corp. to conclude that the leads were extended with the intention to deceive. Microscopic inspection revealed that different revision numbers of the die and differences in various die markings were found even though the samples were advertised to be from the same lot and date code. Commonly, components manufactured within the same date and lot code will have the same die revisions. According to SMT Corp.'s report, the manufacturer also stated that "it is very unusual to have two die runs in a common assembly lot. This is suspicious." Finally, the devices found in the first lot tested went into "last time buy" status—an end-of-life designation—on September 4, 2001, meaning that the parts were misrepresented as newer than they actually were. The manufacturer confirmed this status and added that the part marking did not match its marking scheme, meaning that the date code marked on the samples would not be possible.

*YCC7 (two parts purchased).* Both purchases made using part number YCC7 contained samples that failed several authentication analyses, leading SMT Corp. to conclude that the parts were suspect counterfeit. Both parts were purchased from different vendors using the same part number. An authentic part with this part number is a memory chip that has been used in at least 41 different DOD weapons systems, including the ballistic missile early warning system, the Air Force's Peacekeeper missile and B-1B aircraft, the Navy's Trident submarine and Arleigh Burke class of guided missile destroyer, and the Marine Corps's Harrier aircraft. Failure of the chip, if not redundant, could pose risk to the overall system.

The part we received from one vendor failed four of seven authentication analyses. Visual inspection identified numerous issues, including bent or misshapen leads and lead ends and deformed, less-detailed logos of the claimed manufacturer. X-ray analysis revealed that various parts in the samples contained different sized die. SEM analysis showed that surface material had been precisely removed to allow for re-marking. Finally, delidding of two samples revealed die that were marked from a competitor manufacturer with a different part number than the one we requested. In addition, one die was marked with a 1986 copyright, while the other was labeled 1992.

The part received from the second vendor failed four of nine authentication analyses. Visual inspection showed evidence of remarking, with the color of the top surfaces of samples not matching the color of the bottom surfaces. Some samples displayed faded markings while others were blank and had heavy scuff marks to suggest resurfacing. The markings were also not as clear and consistently placed as manufacturer-etched markings would be. Leads were substandard in quality, had been refurbished, and were not as thick as specified. Further, SEM showed evidence of lapping. Finally, the samples responded inconsistently to Dynasolve testing.

## Category 2: Authentic Part Numbers with Postproduction Date Codes

Similarly, all five of the parts we received and tested after requesting legitimate part numbers but specifying postproduction date codes were also suspected counterfeit, according to SMT Corp. By fulfilling our requests, the four vendors that provided these parts represented them as several years newer than the date the parts were last manufactured, as verified by the part manufacturers. Figure 3 provides photos and detailed test results.

*DAA6 (one part purchased).* The purchase made using part number DAA6 contained samples that failed four of seven authentication analyses, leading SMT Corp. to conclude that the part was suspect counterfeit. Surfaces on the parts in the evidence lots were found to have scratches similar to suspect counterfeit devices that have been remarked, as confirmed by both visual inspection and SEM analysis. In addition, the quality of exterior markings, including a lack of consistency between the manufacturer's logo, was lower than would be expected for authentic devices.

| Category 2<br>Requested authentic part numbers with postproduction date codes (date codes after the last date the part was manufactured) |  |  |  |  |  |
|---|---|---|---|---|---|
| **Analysis performed** | **DAA6** | **IHH1** | **MLL1** | **YCC7** | **YCC7** |
| Visual Inspection | Fail ☒ | Fail ☒ | Fail ☒ | Fail ☒ | Fail ☒ |
| Resistance to Solvents (RTS) and Scrape Test | N/A | Fail ☒ | N/A | Fail ☒ | Fail ☒ |
| Package Configuration and Dimensions | Pass ☑ | Pass ☑ | Pass ☑ | Pass ☑ | Pass ☑ |
| X-Ray Florescence Elemental Analysis | Fail ☒ | Pass ☑ | Fail ☒ | Pass ☑ | Pass ☑ |
| Real-Time X-ray Analysis | Pass ☑ | Fail ☒ | Pass ☑ | Pass ☑ | Pass ☑ |
| Scanning Electron Microscopy (SEM) Analysis | Fail ☒ | Fail ☒ | Fail ☒ | Fail ☒ | Fail ☒ |
| Solderability Test | Pass ☑ | Fail ☒ | Pass ☑ | Pass ☑ | Pass ☑ |
| Dynasolve Test | N/A | Fail ☒ | N/A | N/A | Pass ☑ |
| Delidding and Die Microscopy | Fail ☒ | Fail ☒ | Fail ☒ | Pass ☑ | Pass ☑ |
| **Suspect counterfeit** | **Yes** | **Yes** | **Yes** | **Yes** | **Yes** |

Source: GAO analysis of SMT test results.

Note: Part numbers shown have been altered from the part numbers used for purchasing. N/A Indicated that the analysis was not performed because the unique properties of the part render the test inapplicable or prevent the test from being performed.

Figure 3. Authentication Analysis Results of Part with Invalid Date Codes.

Tooling marks were also found on the bottom of all components within the evidence lot; these marks suggest that the components were pulled from a working environment. Further inspection led SMT Corp. to conclude that many samples with refurbished leads were extended with the intention to deceive. Moreover, XRF analysis revealed the leads contain no lead (Pb) instead of the 3 percent lead (Pb) required by military specifications.[12] Delidding revealed that the die, while correct for this device, were inconsistent. As previously stated, multiple die runs are considered suspicious. Finally, some of the samples went into "last time buy" status in 2001, despite the fact that we requested parts from 2005 or later and the vendor agreed to provide parts from 2010 or later.

*IHH1 (one part purchased).* The purchase made using part number IHH1 contained samples that failed seven of nine authentication analyses, leading SMT Corp. to conclude that the part was suspect counterfeit. The part we received was supplied by a different vendor than the one that supplied the IHH1 part shown in figure 2. Visual inspection revealed numerous issues, including mismatching surface colors, many scratches and scuffs, foreign debris, and leads that were not uniformly aligned. SEM also showed evidence of lapping. RTS testing resulted in removal of resurfacing material, and surfaces faded when exposed to Dynasolve, which should not occur. Further, samples did not solder properly. Finally, X-rays indicated that different die were used within the samples. This was confirmed in delidding, which revealed inconsistencies in size, shape, and date markings. Of the two types of die found in the sample, one does not match the authentic part number.

*MLL1 (one part purchased).* The purchase made using part number MLL1 contained samples that failed four of seven authentication analyses, leading SMT Corp. to conclude that the part was suspect counterfeit. The part we received was supplied by a different vendor than the ones who supplied the MLL1 parts shown in figure 2. Visual inspection revealed scuffs and scratches indicative of re-marking, which was also seen in SEM analysis. Different colored epoxy seals and variegated sizes and colors of the center mounting slug were also seen. Leads also showed evidence of being refurbished with the intent to deceive. XRF testing of the samples revealed that the leads contain no lead (Pb); according to military performance standards, leads should be alloyed with at least 3 percent of lead (Pb).[13] Delidding revealed that die, though similar, had markings indicating different revisions, which is uncommon for die manufactured in the same date code. Finally, the devices went into "last time buy" status in 2001, whereas the tested parts showed a date code indicating they were made in 2008. The manufacturer confirmed this status.

*YCC7 (two parts purchased).* The two purchases made from different vendors using part number YCC7 contained samples that failed several authentication analyses, leading SMT Corp. to conclude that they were suspect counterfeit. The part we received from one vendor failed three of eight authentication analyses. Visual inspection identified numerous issues, including different colored surfaces that suggest re-marking and unknown residues that indicate improper handling or storage. SEM analysis showed that surface material had been precisely removed to allow for re-marking, similarly to a YCC7 part with legitimate date codes tested above. Further, according to the manufacturer, the legitimate version of this part was last shipped in 2003, whereas the tested part showed a manufacturing date code of 2006. RTS testing resulted in removal of the part marking.

The part received from the second vendor failed three of nine authentication analyses. Visual inspection detected numerous issues, including different colored surfaces that suggest re-marking. The markings were also substandard, lacking clarity and consistency in placement. RTS testing removed part markings, further suggesting remarking. SEM showed evidence of lapping. Delidding revealed die that were consistent with the authentic part, but the date code showed evidence of re-marking to make them appear as if they had come from a homogenous lot. Finally, the manufacturer verified that it last shipped this part in 2003, whereas our samples were marked 2007, which according to SMT Corp., could not be possible.

## Category 3: Bogus Part Numbers

We received offers from 40 vendors in China to supply parts using invalid part numbers, and we purchased four parts from four vendors to determine whether they would in fact supply bogus parts. (See fig. 4.) These were different vendors than the ones that supplied us with the suspect counterfeit parts. The invalid numbers were based on actual part numbers, but certain portions that define a part's performance specifications were changed. For example, one of our invalid numbers was for an actual voltage regulator but that operated at bogus specifications. None of the invalid part numbers were listed in DLA's Federal Logistics Information System and, according to selected manufacturers, none are associated with parts that have ever been manufactured. As such, we did not send the parts to SMT Corp. for authentication analysis.

We received the four bogus parts after requesting invalid part numbers DAA5, GDD4, and 3MM8. We made two orders using DAA5, one from each Internet purchasing platform, which were fulfilled by different vendors. The parts we received from each vendor appeared similar, as shown in figure 4. The similarity may be due to a number of factors. For example, the vendors could have simply ignored the invalid portion of the part numbers we requested (they did not contact us to inform us that the numbers were invalid). Another possible explanation could be that the parts happened to be fulfilled by the same vendor operating under two different names.

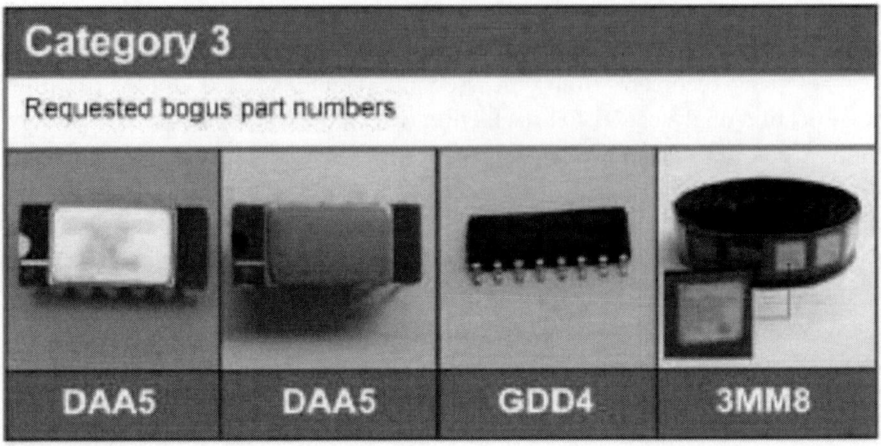


Source: GAO.

Note: Part number shown have been altered from the part numbers used for purchasing.

Figure 4. Photos of Parts Received Despite Request for Invalid Part Numbers.

In furtherance of our investigation to determine the willingness of firms to provide us bogus parts, we created a totally fictitious part number that was not based on an actual part number and requested quotations over one Internet platform. We received an offer to supply the part from one vendor, but did not invest the resources to purchase the bogus part.

Richard J. Hillman
Managing Director
Forensic Audits and Investigative Service

Timothy Persons
Chief Scientist
U.S. Government Accountability Office

## APPENDIX I: DETAILS OF AUTHENTICATION ANALYSIS TESTS

This appendix provides details on each of the tests that constitute the authentication analysis SMT Corp. conducted for the parts we purchased.

*Visual inspection:* Visual inspection is performed on a predetermined number of samples (usually 100 percent) to look for legitimate nonconformance issues as well as any red flags commonly found within suspect counterfeit devices.

*Resistance to solvents (RTS):* A mixture of mineral spirits and isopropyl alcohol is used to determine the part marking resistance and pure acetone is used to remove any resurface material. This test is not performed on all parts. In some cases, resurfacing material would not be used by counterfeiters to re-mark a part; in others, the solvents would remove markings even on legitimate parts.

*X-ray florescence (XRF) elemental analysis:* The XRF gathers and measures the elements within a target area. This is used specifically for testing components for RoHS or Hi-Rel conformance, which refer to dangerous substances such as lead (Pb), cadmium (Cd), and mercury (Hg) that are commonly used in electronics manufacturing. For suspect counterfeit devices, it helps determine if a component has the correct plating for the specification it supposed to adhere to.

*Package configuration and dimensions:* This test measures key areas of the device to see if they fall within industry specifications.

*Real-time X-ray analysis:* X-ray analysis is performed on a predetermined number of samples (usually 100 percent). The internal construction of components is inspected (depending on the component package type) for legitimate issues such as broken/taut bond wires, electrostatic discharge damage, broken die, and so forth. For suspect counterfeit devices, the differences in die size/shape, lead frames, bond wire layout, and so forth are inspected.

*Scanning electron microscopy:* A scanning electron microscope is used to perform an exterior visual inspection—more in depth than the previous visual inspection. This is usually performed on a two-piece sample from the evidence lot. Depending on the package type, indications of suspect counterfeit devices are sought, including surface lapping, sandblasting, and sanding with regard to part marking removal.

*Solderability:* This test is usually for legitimate components to determine if they will solder properly when they are used in production.

*Dynasolve:* Dynasolve is a chemical used to break down epoxies in an effort to remove resurfacing material that is impervious to the standard RTS test.

*Decapsulation/delidding and die verification:* The die of a component is exposed with either corrosive materials or a cutting apparatus. This is done to inspect the die or "brain" of a component to determine its legitimacy. This process is performed on numerous samples to look for differences between samples, such as die metallization layout, revisions, part numbers, and so forth—all of which are red flags for suspect counterfeit parts.

## End Notes

[1] GAO, Defense Supplier Base: DOD Should Leverage Ongoing Initiatives in Developing Its Program to Mitigate Risk of Counterfeit Parts, GAO-10-389 (Washington, D.C.: Mar. 29, 2010).

[2] GAO, Space and Missile Defense Acquisitions: Periodic Assessment Needed to Correct Parts Quality Problems in Major Programs, GAO-11-404 (Washington, D.C.: June 24, 2011).

[3] GAO, DOD Supply Chain: Preliminary Observations Indicate That Counterfeit Electronic Parts Can Be Found on Internet Purchasing Platforms, GAO-12-213T (Washington, D.C.: Nov. 8, 2011).

[4] The Central Contractor Registration is the primary contractor registrant database for the U.S. federal government. The Central Contractor Registration collects, validates, stores, and disseminates data in support of agency acquisition missions.

[5] DLA's Federal Logistics Information System via the World Wide Web provides general information about more than 8 million supply items used by the U.S. government and North Atlantic Treaty Organization (NATO) allies.

[6] We selected SMT Corp. as the independent, full component authentication testing laboratory based on its (1) ability to conduct 100 percent component inspection with transmission X-rays, (2) use of a patented heated solvent test, and (3) use of scanning electron microscopy to detect surface abnormalities as well as doing spectroscopic analysis of surface material on the components.

[7] These vendors usually responded to our initial requests for quotes within a day.

[8] XRF analyzers quickly and nondestructively determine the elemental composition of materials commonly found in microelectronic devices. Each of the elements present in a sample produces a unique set of characteristic x-rays that reveals the chemistry of the sample in a manner analogous to a fingerprint. A lead is an electrical connection consisting of a length of wire or soldering pad that comes from a device. Leads are used for physical support, to transfer power, to probe circuits, and to transmit information.

[9] DOD, DOD Performance Specification for Integrated Circuits (Microcircuits) Manufacturing, MIL-PRF-38535J (Dec. 28, 2010).

[10] A die is a small wafer of semiconducting material on which a functional circuit is fabricated.

[11] DOD, DOD Performance Specification for Integrated Circuits (Microcircuits) Manufacturing.

[12] DOD, DOD Performance Specification for Integrated Circuits (Microcircuits) Manufacturing.

[13] DOD, DOD Performance Specification for Integrated Circuits (Microcircuits) Manufacturing.

In: Counterfeit Parts
Editor: Erik Dawson
ISBN: 978-1-63485-989-9


*Chapter 3*

# DEFENSE SUPPLIER BASE: DOD SHOULD LEVERAGE ONGOING INITIATIVES IN DEVELOPING ITS PROGRAM TO MITIGATE RISK OF COUNTERFEIT PARTS*

*United States Government Accountability Office*

## ABBREVIATIONS

| | |
|---|---|
| DCMA | Defense Contract Management Agency |
| DLA | Defense Logistics Agency |
| DOD | Department of Defense |
| GIDEP | Government Industry Data Exchange Program |
| HMMWV | High Mobility Multi-purpose Wheeled Vehicles |
| JDRS | Joint Deficiency Reporting System |
| Joint STARS | Joint Surveillance Target Attack Radar System |
| MDA | Missile Defense Agency |
| OCM | Original Component Manufacturer |
| PDREP | Product Data Reporting and Evaluation Program |

* This is an edited, reformatted and augmented version of The United States Government Accountability Office publication, GAO-10-389, dated March 2010.

## Why GAO Did This Study

Counterfeit parts—generally those whose sources knowingly misrepresent the parts' identity or pedigree—have the potential to seriously disrupt the Department of Defense (DOD) supply chain, delay missions, and affect the integrity of weapon systems. Almost anything is at risk of being counterfeited, from fasteners used on aircraft to electronics used on missile guidance systems. Further, there can be many sources of counterfeit parts as DOD draws from a large network of global suppliers.

Based on a congressional request, GAO examined (1) DOD's knowledge of counterfeit parts in its supply chain, (2) DOD processes to detect and prevent counterfeit parts, and (3) commercial initiatives to mitigate the risk of counterfeit parts.

GAO's findings are based on an examination of DOD regulations, guidance, and databases used to track deficient parts, as well as a Department of Commerce study on counterfeit parts; interviews with Commerce, DOD, and commercial-sector officials at selected locations; and a review of planned and existing efforts for counterfeit-part mitigation.

## What GAO Recommends

GAO recommends that DOD leverage existing initiatives to establish anticounterfeiting guidance and disseminate this guidance to all DOD components and defense contractors. DOD concurred with each of the recommendations.

## What GAO Found

DOD is limited in its ability to determine the extent to which counterfeit parts exist in its supply chain because it does not have a departmentwide definition of the term "counterfeit" and a consistent means to identify instances of suspected counterfeit parts. While some DOD entities have developed their own definitions, these can vary in scope. Further, two DOD databases that track deficient parts—those that do not conform to standards—are not designed to track counterfeit parts. A third governmentwide database can track suspected counterfeit parts, but according to officials, reporting is low due to the perceived legal implications of reporting prior to a full investigation. Nonetheless, officials we met with across DOD cited instances of counterfeit parts, as shown in the table below. A recent Department of Commerce study also identified the existence of counterfeit electronic parts within DOD and industry supply chains. DOD is in the early stages of developing a program to help mitigate the risks of counterfeit parts.

**Examples of Counterfeit Parts in DOD's Supply Chain**

| Part | Description |
|---|---|
| GPS oscillators | The Air Force and Navy use these oscillators for navigation onover 4,000 systems. Part failure could affect the mission of certain systems. |
| Self-locking nuts | Self-locking nuts, used in aviation braking, were cracking. |
| Titanium | The supplier sold substandard titanium, used in fighter jet engine mounts. |
| Brake shoes | Brake shoes were made with substandard materials, including seaweed. |

Source: DOD.

DOD does not currently have a policy or specific processes for detecting and preventing counterfeit parts. Existing procurement and quality-control practices used to identify deficient parts are limited in their ability to prevent and detect counterfeit parts in DOD's supply chain. For example, several DOD weapon system program and logistics officials told us that staff responsible for assembling and repairing equipment are not trained to identify counterfeit parts. Some DOD components and prime defense contractors have taken initial steps to mitigate the risk of counterfeit parts, such as creating risk-assessment tools and implementing a new electronic parts standard.

Also facing risks from counterfeit parts, individual commercial sector companies have developed a number of anticounterfeiting measures, including increased supplier visibility, detection, reporting, and disposal. Recent collaborative industry initiatives have focused on identifying and sharing methods to reduce the likelihood of counterfeit parts entering the supply chain. Because many of the commercial sector companies produce items similar to those used by DOD, agency officials have an opportunity to leverage knowledge and ongoing and planned initiatives to help mitigate the risk of counterfeit parts as DOD develops its anticounterfeiting strategy.

March 29, 2010

The Honorable Sherrod Brown
Chairman
Subcommittee on Economic Policy
Committee on Banking, Housing, and Urban Affairs
United States Senate

The Honorable Evan Bayh
Chairman
Subcommittee on Security and International Trade and Finance
Committee on Banking, Housing, and Urban Affairs
United States Senate

DOD draws from a large network of global suppliers and manages over 4 million different parts at a cost of over $94 billion; therefore, counterfeit parts can enter its supply chain.[1] Almost anything is at risk of being counterfeited including fasteners used on aircraft, electronics used on missile guidance systems, and materials used in body armor and engine mounts. Counterfeit parts have the potential to cause a serious disruption to DOD supply chains, delay ongoing missions, and even affect the integrity of weapon systems. Counterfeits are not limited to the DOD supply chain and exist in other government entities, such as the National Aeronautics and Space Administration and the Department of Energy, as well as in many commercial settings as diverse as software, commercial aviation, automotive parts, and consumer electronics and can threaten the safety of consumers.

On the basis of your interest in DOD's ability to detect and prevent counterfeit parts, we examined (1) the extent of DOD's knowledge of counterfeit parts in its supply chain, (2) DOD processes to detect and prevent counterfeit parts, and (3) commercial initiatives to mitigate the risk of counterfeit parts in their supply chains.

To conduct our work, we reviewed regulations, guidelines, and databases to determine how DOD defines and tracks counterfeit parts. We interviewed senior DOD headquarters officials, as well as weapon system program and logistics officials from the Army, Navy, Air Force, Missile Defense Agency (MDA), and Defense Logistics Agency (DLA) about their knowledge of the counterfeit parts problem and instances of counterfeits. We also reviewed a Department of Commerce study of counterfeit electronic parts and met with officials to discuss their findings. To identify practices for preventing and detecting counterfeit parts, we selected and reviewed a nongeneralizable sample of 16 weapon systems representing a mix of aerospace, ground vehicle, and missile defense sectors with mature technologies. We identified initiatives planned and practices used by DOD and defense contractors to prevent and detect counterfeit parts. To identify commercial practices used to mitigate the risk of procuring counterfeit parts, we interviewed officials from selected companies and associations within the automotive, aviation, and electronics industries— sectors that have experienced counterfeit parts in their supply chains or produce items similar to those used by the DOD programs we reviewed. For more on our scope and methodology, see appendix I. We performed our review from January 2009 through March 2010, in accordance with generally accepted government auditing standards. Those standards require that we plan and perform the audit to obtain sufficient, appropriate evidence to provide a reasonable basis for our findings and conclusions based on our audit objectives. We believe that the evidence obtained provides a reasonable basis for our findings and conclusions based on our audit objectives.

## BACKGROUND

Generally, the term counterfeit refers to instances in which the identity or pedigree of a product is knowingly misrepresented by individuals or companies. Counterfeiters often try to take advantage of the established worth of the imitated product, and the counterfeit product may not work as well as the genuine article. The threat of counterfeit parts continues to grow as counterfeiters have developed more sophisticated capabilities to replicate parts and gain access to scrap materials that were thought to have been destroyed. Counterfeiters exist across industries and are able to respond to changes in market conditions. Counterfeit parts can be quickly distributed in online markets. Almost every industry can be affected by counterfeit parts.

Counterfeiting can affect the safety, operational readiness, costs, and the critical nature of the military mission. DOD procures millions of parts through its logistics support providers—DLA supply centers, military service depots, and defense contractors—who are responsible for ensuring the reliability of the DOD parts they procure. As they draw from a large network of suppliers in an increasingly global supply chain, there can be limited visibility into these sources and greater risk of procuring counterfeit parts. Also, as DOD weapon systems age, products required to support it may no longer be available from the original manufacturers or through franchised or authorized suppliers but could be available from independent distributors, brokers, or aftermarket manufacturers. Parts and components bought by DOD can come from different types of suppliers, as shown in table 1.

**Table 1. Types of DOD Suppliers of Parts and Components**

| Type of source | Description |
|---|---|
| Original component manufacturer (OCM) | Organization that designs, or engineers, or both, a part and is pursuing or has obtained the intellectual property rights to that part. |
| Franchised distributor | Distributor with which OCM has a contractual agreement to buy, stock, repackage, sell and distribute its product lines. |
| Independent distributor | Distributor that purchases new parts with theintention to sell and redistribute them back into the market, and which does not have contractual agreements with OCM. |
| Broker / broker distributor | In the independent distribution market, brokers are professionally referred to as independent distributors. A broker distributoris a type of independent distributor that works in a just-in-time environment by searching the industry and locating parts for customers. |
| Aftermarket manufacturer | Manufacturer that either produces and sells replacement parts authorized by the OCM, or produces parts through emulation, reverse-engineering, or redesign that match OCM specifications and satisfy customer needs without violating OCM intellectual property rights, patents, or copyrights. |

Source: GAO summary of SAE International data.

Note: The definitions are based on SAE Aerospace Standard 5553, Counterfeit Electronic Parts; Avoidance, Detection, Mitigation and Disposition, issued in April 2009.

# The Extent of Counterfeit Parts in DOD's Supply Chain Is Unknown

## DOD Does Not Have a Common Definition for Counterfeit Parts

DOD lacks a departmentwide definition of the term counterfeit. In our discussions with DOD logistics and program officials, several told us they are uncertain how to define counterfeit parts, and many officials also stated that a common definition would be useful. In the absence of a departmentwide definition of counterfeit parts, some DOD entities have developed their own. Although there are similarities among these definitions, the scope varies. For example, one DLA supply center defined a part as counterfeit only when it misrepresented the part's trademark. In contrast, a different DLA supply center defined counterfeit parts more broadly to include misrepresentations of a part's quality and performance. In August 2009, DOD endorsed an aerospace standard created by SAE International that includes a definition of the term counterfeit part.[2] While this standard is available departmentwide, it is left to the discretion of each DOD program as to whether it wants to use the standard. Some DOD officials who support aviation programs, such as the F-15, told us they were using or considering use of the standard, while other DOD officials told us they were unaware of it. Others were uncertain how it would apply beyond avionics to components like fasteners, uniforms, tires, and brake pads. In some cases, officials stated the definition is too broad for their use.

## DOD Databases Do Not Capture Data on Counterfeit Parts

The two primary databases DOD uses to report deficient parts—the Product Data Reporting and Evaluation Program (PDREP) and the Joint Deficiency Reporting System (JDRS)[3]—have data fields that enable users primarily to track information on deficient parts, but neither is designed specifically to track counterfeit parts. DOD considers products that do not conform to quality or design specifications to be deficient.[4] Both of these systems allow users to enter a cause code for why a part is deficient, but neither database has a code to capture the deficiency as counterfeit. As a result, users are limited to reporting a suspected counterfeit part in narrative descriptions. However, identifying instances of counterfeit parts through searches of narrative descriptions is difficult due to a lack of common terminology. For example, an Air Force official told us that when he searched the JDRS system, he found 3 out of more than 94,000 entries that discussed counterfeit parts. We performed similar searches and found that the terms associated with counterfeit are rarely included in narrative fields. In consultation with database managers from both PDREP and JDRS, we developed a list of 11 terms associated with counterfeit parts and searched the systems' narrative fields for these terms over a 5-year period ranging from October 1, 2004, to September 30, 2009.[5] We found that less than 1 percent of the reports in the databases included one of our search terms, and a manual review of these cases determined that only a few were relevant to counterfeit parts.

DOD entities also have access to the Government Industry Data Exchange Program (GIDEP)—a Web-based database—that allows government and industry participants to share information on deficient parts, including counterfeit. Specifically, a GIDEP user can submit information on a suspected counterfeit part and GIDEP policy allows for up to 15 days for the supplier to respond before posting this information to the database. A 1991 Office of Management and Budget policy letter instructs government agencies to use GIDEP to report deficient[6] parts. However, the GIDEP Deputy Program Manager told us that GIDEP is not widely used to report suspect counterfeits. He stated that the policy letter was intended as a short-term requirement for government use of GIDEP until a Federal Acquisition Regulation change was made, which never occurred. He further stated that DOD had previously issued a military standard[7] requiring use of GIDEP, which was canceled during acquisition reform in 1996. DOD logistical support providers and contractors that we spoke with cited concerns with using the GIDEP system such as delayed reporting, liability issues, and effect on criminal investigations.

- Delayed Reporting: A 15-day delay in posting reports to the system allows suppliers to investigate and respond to reports concerning their products. However, during this time, a counterfeit part could continue to be used or purchased.[8]
- Liability Issues: Some officials expressed concerns about the legal implications of reporting a part as suspect counterfeit before it had been proven. Fear of lawsuits was repeatedly cited as a reason cases are not reported to GIDEP.
- Effect on Investigations: Another concern officials raised about reporting cases to GIDEP is the possibility of alerting suppliers to active

investigations, as investigators may want to monitor a supplier's activities to gather further evidence of possible illegal activity.

## Counterfeit Parts Have Been Found in DOD's Supply Chain

In the absence of data collected on counterfeit parts, we visited military services, MDA, DLA, selected defense contractors, and suppliers; many of these officials provided specific examples of counterfeit or suspect counterfeit parts. As definitions of "counterfeit" vary within DOD, they generally refer to instances in which individuals or companies knowingly misrepresent the identity or pedigree of a part. Specific examples of the types of counterfeits encountered by DOD include

- parts falsely claimed by the supplier to be from a particular manufacturer,
- parts that deliberately do not contain the proper internal components or construction consistent with the ordered part,
- authentic parts whose age or treatment have been knowingly misrepresented, and
- parts with fake packaging.

We met with DOD program officials and logistical support providers across 16 DOD programs and three DLA supply centers and discussed instances of suspect and confirmed counterfeit parts; examples are shown in appendix II. About two-thirds of these instances involved fasteners or electronic parts while the remainder included materials ranging from titanium used in aircraft engine mounts to Kevlar used in body armor plates. The following illustrates the examples of counterfeit parts and actions taken provided by officials across DOD.

Army

- *Seatbelt clasps*: Seatbelt parts were made from a grade of aluminum that was inferior to that specified in DOD's requirements. The parts were found to be deficient when the seatbelts were accidentally dropped and they broke.

Navy

- *Seatbelt clasps:* Seatbelt parts were made from a grade of aluminum that was inferior to that specified in DOD's requirements. The parts were found to be deficient when the seatbelts were accidentally dropped and they broke.

Air Force

- *Microprocessor:* The Air Force needed microprocessors that were no longer produced by the original manufacturer for its F-15 flight-control computer. These microprocessors were procured from a broker and F15 technicians noticed additional markings on the microprocessor and character spacing inconsistent with the original part. A total of four counterfeit microprocessors were found and as a result were not installed on the F-15's operational flight control computers.
- *Global Positioning System:* Oscillators used for navigation on over 4,000 Air Force and Navy systems experienced a high failure rate and failed a retest. These oscillators were provided by a supplier that Global Positioning System engineers had previously disapproved as a supply source. Air Force officials stated that while the failure would not cause a safety-of-flight issue, it could prevent some unmanned systems from returning from their missions.

MDA

- *Operational Amplifiers***:** A counterfeit operational amplifier, which can be used on multiple MDA systems, was identified on MDA hardware during testing. The failed part was found on a circuit board supplied by a subcontractor. It was later determined that the subcontractor purchased these parts from a parts broker who was not authorized to distribute parts by the original component manufacturer. To date, all parts have been accounted for and secured from further use on any other products.
- *Microcircuits:* A counterfeit microcircuit, which can be used on multiple MDA systems, was identified on MDA hardware. MDA's visual inspection showed that the part was resurfaced and remarked, which prompted authenticity testing. Tests revealed surface scratches, inconsistencies in the part marking, and evidence of tampering. These parts were purchased from a parts broker who was not authorized to distribute parts by the original component manufacturer.

DLA

- *Packaging and small parts:* During a 2-year period, a supplier and three coconspirators packaged hundreds of commercial items from hardware and consumer electronics

> stores and labeled them as military-grade items. For example, the supplier placed a rubber washer from a local hardware store in a package labeled as a brass washer for use on a submarine. The supplier also labeled the package containing a circuit from a personal computer as a $7,000 circuit for a missile guidance system. The suppliers avoided detection by labeling packages to appear authentic, even though they contained the wrong part. The supplier received $3 million from contracts totaling $8 million before fleeing the country. He has been extradited to the United States and awaits trial; his coconspirators have been convicted.

The Department of Commerce also identified the existence of counterfeit parts in DOD's supply chain in a study released in January 2010.[9] This study, sponsored by Naval Air Systems Command, was designed to provide statistics on the extent of infiltration of counterfeit electronic components into the United States industrial and supply chains, to understand how different segments of the supply chain currently address the issue, and to gather best practices from the supply chain on how to handle counterfeits. The department received completed surveys from 387 respondents representing five segments in the U.S. supply chain—OCMs, distributors and brokers, circuit-board assemblers, prime contractors and subcontractors, and DOD entities. The surveys included questions addressing past experiences with counterfeit parts and practices used in identifying them. While the study did not provide a number for the total counterfeit incidents at DOD, it noted that 14 DOD organizations had reported incidents of counterfeit parts. The study's survey respondents identified a growth in incidents of counterfeit parts across the electronics industry from about 3,300 in 2005 to over 8,000 incidents in 2008. Survey respondents attributed this growth to a number of factors, such as a growth in the number of counterfeit parts, better detection methods, and improved tracking of counterfeit incidents.

## DOD Is in the Early Stages of Gathering Information on the Counterfeit Parts Problem

In April 2009 DOD formed a departmentwide team—partially in response to media reports that highlighted the existence of counterfeit parts in the DOD supply chain[10]—to collect information and recommend actions to mitigate the risk of counterfeit parts in its supply chain. Standing participants include representatives from DOD's Office of the Under Secretary of Defense for Acquisition, Technology & Logistics, DLA, the Defense Contract Management Agency, the Defense Standardization Program Office, MDA, and military law enforcement and investigative agencies.[11] The team also incorporates liaisons from groups such as the defense industry, Defense Intelligence Agency, Federal Aviation Administration, National Aeronautics and Space Administration, Department of Energy, Department of Commerce, and state and federal law enforcement organizations.

To gather preliminary information on the counterfeit problem in DOD, the team has visited three DOD facilities to observe operations and discuss occurrences of and problems with counterfeit in the supply chain. The team plans to complete a review of current DOD processes and procedures for the handling and storage, detection, disposal, and reporting of counterfeit parts by July 2010. The team then plans to assess the policies, procedures, and metrics needed to address the issue of counterfeit parts . Additionally, the team is developing training materials that it plans to make available through the Defense Acquisition University, to increase the general awareness of counterfeit parts and plans to develop additional training on detection techniques.

# DOD's Existing Practices Are Limited in Protecting Its Supply Chain against Counterfeit Parts

## DOD Relies on Existing Procurement and Quality Control Practices That Are Not Specifically Designed to Address Counterfeit Parts

DOD relies on existing procurement and quality control practices to ensure the quality of the parts in its supply chain. However, these practices are not designed to specifically address counterfeit parts. Limitations in the areas of obtaining supplier visibility, investigating part deficiencies, and reporting and disposal may reduce DOD's ability to mitigate risks posed by counterfeit parts.

Obtaining supplier visibility: DOD and its prime contractors rely on suppliers across a global supply chain for parts and materials. Federal acquisition regulations require that agency contracting officers consider whether a supplier is responsible before awarding a contract and note that the award of a contract to a supplier based on the lowest price alone can result in additional costs if there is subsequent default, late deliveries, or other unsatisfactory performance.[12] While cost or price is always a consideration when purchasing goods, an abnormally low price, especially from an unfamiliar source, can be an indication that there is a need to assess the supplier's ability to meet the requirements of the contract. For example, a DLA contracting official described an instance in which a supplier new to DLA was awarded a contract based on a low price and a performance score of 100 percent. However, the score was misleading as the supplier had no past performance to measure. Ultimately, the supplier was unable to meet the requirements of the contract. Further, DOD parts can be purchased through the use of automated systems that have limited visibility on suppliers and can increase the risk of purchasing counterfeit parts. To address the risks of using automated source selection, DLA has a pilot project to create a list of qualified distributors for the supply of two electronic items—semiconductors and microcircuits. Of the 53 distributors that applied, 13 were selected based on their qualifications. DLA plans to review other parts to determine if the pilot can be expanded. In addition, DOD has a number of weapons systems that have remained in service longer than expected—such as the B-52 bomber—and require parts that are no longer available from the original manufacturer or its authorized distributors. When parts are needed for these systems, they are often provided by brokers or independent distributors. As buying from these sources reduces DOD's visibility into a part's pedigree, additional steps are required in assuring that the part is reliable or authentic.

Detecting Part Deficiencies: DOD can have a part's quality and authenticity tested through destructive and nondestructive methods prior to awarding a contract. However, several DOD officials told us that staff responsible for assembling and repairing systems and equipment may not have the expertise to identify suspect counterfeit parts outside of those that demonstrate performance failures because they are not trained to identify counterfeit parts and have limited awareness of the issue. In addition, DOD contracting officials told us that the cost and time associated with testing may be prohibitive, especially for lower-cost parts such as a 50-cent fastener. Other factors were cited by DOD officials at several testing centers as limitations such as the barriers to testing parts that are only available in limited quantities or are expensive. For instance, the F-15 program was in need of two spare parts, but only two of these parts were available in the supply chain, so the preferred destructive testing could not be performed.

Reporting and disposal: Generally, DOD has processes in place for reporting and disposal of deficient parts. Reporting of a deficient part that is suspected to be counterfeit enables further investigation to confirm that a part is counterfeit. As described above, DOD uses JDRS and PDREP to report deficient parts, but does not have a specific field in these databases to report counterfeit parts. Some DOD officials stated that they report suspect counterfeits to internal fraud teams, others indicated that they would contact local law enforcement or the Federal Bureau of Investigation in similar cases. DOD officials told us that when they found counterfeit parts they have shared this information through informal methods such as e-mails or phone calls. Others, such as MDA, use formal methods to convey this information such as bulletins that alert MDA staff of counterfeiting techniques and how to detect them as well as advisories on confirmed counterfeit parts found in MDA programs. MDA officials stated that these methods are an effective way to immediately alert their staff of counterfeit parts.

Further, depending on the condition of a noncounterfeit, deficient part and its related demilitarization code, it can be refurbished, resold, or destroyed. The disposal of counterfeit and scrapped parts is an area of vulnerability as they could reenter the supply chain. According to officials from the Defense Reutilization and Marketing Service—the agency responsible for destroying and disposing of DOD's excess and surplus parts—it is critical that a part and its related demilitarization code be identified as counterfeit when it is sent for disposal to prevent it from reentering DOD's supply chain. However, DOD does not have a consistent method to identify parts as counterfeit when they are sent for disposal. Some parts designated for disposal have made their way back into the supply chain. For example, DOD program officials described a helicopter part that had the same serial number as a defective one that had been destroyed. An X-ray test revealed the destroyed part had been welded back together and put back in DOD's inventory.

## Some DOD Components and Contractors Have Taken Initial Steps to Address Counterfeit Parts

In the absence of a departmentwide policy, some DOD components and their contractors have supplemented existing procurement and quality-control practices to help mitigate the risk of counterfeit parts in the DOD supply chain. For example, MDA has established a 12-person organization that leverages subject-matter expertise at two DOD laboratories to identify, evaluate, and track the effects of counterfeit parts on all MDA hardware. MDA policies to address counterfeits are part of its Parts, Materials, and Processes Mission Assurance Plan which includes instructions on part selection, procurement, receipt, testing, and use of parts. This plan specifically identifies three steps to offset the presence of counterfeit parts and materials in the market: (1) preventing counterfeit parts and materials by using only authorized distributors, with associated certifying paperwork; (2) detecting and containing counterfeit parts and materials through appropriate inspection and test methods; and (3) notifying the user community of potential counterfeit concerns and assisting in prosecution. The plan also instructs programs to impound suspect counterfeit parts and all items from the same lot and to not return suspected counterfeit parts to suppliers, preventing them from being sold to others. According to MDA officials, all new contracts include adherence to the plan's section on counterfeit parts and materials, and MDA has developed policies that can be applied to existing contracts. MDA further has applied DOD's item-unique identification technology that provides for the marking of individual items—whose unit acquisition cost is $5,000 or more—with a set of globally unique data elements. This technology is designed to help DOD value and track items throughout their life cycle by requiring equipment manufacturers to assign unique identification numbers to parts acquired under DOD contracts, thus enabling better traceability of a part to a specific manufacturer. MDA also has an ongoing effort to develop tools to identify, quantify, and manage the risk of counterfeit parts in the supply chain as counterfeits or suspect counterfeits are detected. DLA's Supply Center in Columbus, Ohio, has an established team that investigates suspect counterfeit parts under the broader scope of fraud. The team is composed of members from DLA's product verification, contracting, and legal offices as well as the Defense Criminal Investigative Service and handles cases ranging from part deficiencies to contractor misconduct. When encountering a counterfeit part, the team's analysis of engineering investigations, product testing, and criminal investigations can be used as evidence in criminal and civil cases.

DOD's prime contractors are also independently taking steps to protect the supply chain from counterfeits. As DOD relies on its suppliers to provide weapons, equipment, and raw materials to meet U.S. national security objectives, these activities directly affect DOD's own efforts. Several prime contractors told us that they are using a recently adopted industry standard to develop counterfeit protection plans.[3] The standard provides strategies to mitigate the risks of procuring counterfeit products and standardizes practices to maximize availability of authentic parts and procure parts from reliable sources. Additionally, it standardizes practices to assure the authenticity of parts, control parts that are identified as counterfeit, and report counterfeit parts to other potential users and government investigative authorities. Prime contractors using this standard are also focusing on ensuring traceability within their supply chains through flow-down requirements to subcontractors. For example, one contractor includes a clause in its contracts that states that its suppliers shall ensure that they do not deliver counterfeits but if this occurs, the supplier would immediately notify the defense contractor and assume responsibility for the cost of replacing the counterfeit parts. Several of the companies also provide training on detecting counterfeits within their product lines.

## A Number of Commercial Initiatives Exist to Mitigate the Risk of Counterfeit Parts in Supply Chains

### Companies Have Developed Anticounterfeiting Practices to Address Vulnerabilities to Counterfeit Parts

As supply chains across industries are also vulnerable to the risk of counterfeit parts, we met with selected companies representing commercial aerospace, electronics, and automotive sectors that have taken measures to address the counterfeiting challenges they face. Companies we met with cited procedures and practices that they have incorporated to help mitigate the risk of counterfeit parts in the areas of supplier visibility, detection, and reporting and disposal.

Supplier Visibility: To ensure that parts and materials are reliable, commercial companies we met with described several practices to identify potential sources of counterfeiting activity. These practices include regular assessments of a supplier's internal controls ranging from their access to product designs to manufacturing facility security. Some practices also included instituting extra measures when purchasing from independent distributors such as internal and external validation and testing requirements, and part-authenticity documentation—such as certificates of conformance.

Detection of Counterfeits: Companies we spoke with are using a number of practices to make their products and packaging more difficult to replicate and to increase the opportunities to identify counterfeits in their supply chains. Some companies incorporate rare, proprietary, or expensive materials on parts and packaging, which can deter counterfeiters. Some companies also include markings on products and packaging that, when absent or altered, could alert investigators or consumers to potential counterfeits. One company allows customers to report suspected counterfeits on its Web site and posts pictures of markings and security features for customers and investigators to use in distinguishing genuine from counterfeit products. Companies have also coordinated with the Department of Homeland Security's Customs and Border Protection inspectors to identify counterfeits. One company visited inspectors at two ports that receive a high volume of imports for this company, to inform inspectors of product packaging characteristics and how to easily identify counterfeit packaging. This effort resulted in an increased number of seizures of suspected counterfeit products at these two ports.

Reporting and Disposal of Counterfeits: Several company officials identified the lack of oversight of the scrapping, recycling, and disposal of parts as an avoidable source of counterfeiting. Specific practices that companies use to confirm that scrapped, excess, and suspected counterfeit materials are not used to make more counterfeit parts include

- requiring suspect counterfeits to be quarantined upon detection,
- auditing suppliers to ensure proper tracking of the amount of scrapped material destroyed,
- requiring suppliers to use contract clauses that prevent the resale of scrap parts to third parties, and
- witnessing the destruction of seized or returned counterfeit parts.

## Industry Associations Identify and Share Anticounterfeiting Practices

Several industry associations identify and share counterfeit-mitigation practices. Activities include training, knowledge exchange, and developing standards. These associations can provide a forum for a diverse set of participants to arrive at agreement on collaborative mitigation steps for the counterfeit issue. The recently issued Department of Commerce report on the existence of counterfeit electronics across the industry has also recommended mitigation strategies for counterfeit parts.

In April 2009, SAE International issued Aerospace Standard 5553, "Counterfeit Electronic Parts; Avoidance, Detection, Mitigation and Disposition." The standard was created to provide uniform requirements, practices, and methods to mitigate the risks of receiving and installing counterfeit electronic parts.[14] It also provides guidance for establishing a counterfeit-control plan to include parts availability, purchasing process, product verification, investigation, reporting, and disposal. SAE International is providing training on applying this standard, including a segment on detection and visual inspection of actual counterfeit parts. For example, in its visual inspection segment, the SAE training notes that characteristics of a part that may indicate it is counterfeit include inconsistencies in the part's texture, colors, material, or condition; quality of ink or laser markings; condition of part labels; and markings that include information such as production dates and manufacturing locations. As shown in figure 1, visual inspection of a part's texture can uncover counterfeits that have been resurfaced.

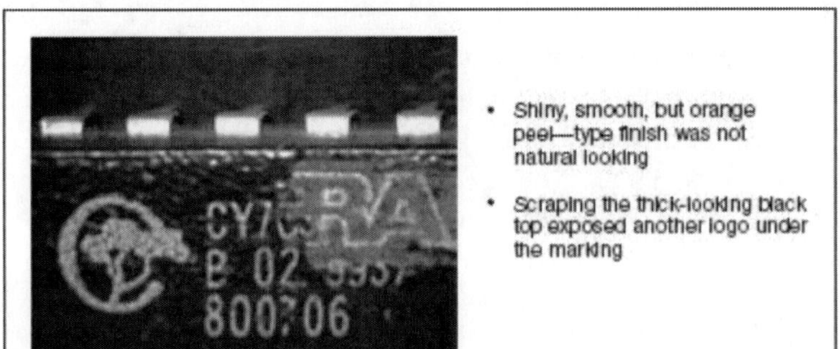


Source: SAE International and the Jet Propulsion Laboratory.
Note: Information is from SAE 5553 Training Manual dated November 2009.

Figure 1. Visual Detection of a Counterfeit Integrated Circuit.

In 2009, a number of conferences were held to facilitate a collaborative dialogue between industry representatives, law enforcement, and government agencies. Specifically, in September, DOD's Defense Standardization Program Office sponsored its annual Diminishing Manufacturing Sources and Material Shortages and Standardization Conference where participants discussed the counterfeit part issue and how to increase awareness across industries. Additionally, in December, the Center for Advanced Life Cycle Engineering hosted its third annual symposium on avoiding, detecting, and preventing counterfeit electronic parts.[15] Sessions at the symposium were aimed at generating awareness of the counterfeit parts issue and sharing the perspectives of law enforcement, supply chain managers, and government. The symposium also provided information on technical tools and methods to detect and prevent counterfeit parts.

In late 2008, the Aerospace Industries Association established an integrated project team across aerospace, space, and defense products to address challenges in the supply chain for mitigating the risk of counterfeit parts. The team worked with government agencies, original manufacturers, industry associations, and independent distributors across three main objectives to: (1) discuss U.S. government acquisition and procurement policies to avoid introducing counterfeit parts and materials into products; (2) create a set of recommendations for government and industry to ensure that the risk of introducing counterfeit parts and materials is minimized, is consistent with risks accepted by the customer, and implementable without sacrificing the benefits of buying commercially available products; and (3) engage the U.S. government in discussions concerning enforcement of policies to avoid the introduction of counterfeit products into the United States. The project team has provided its recommendations to its association members and expects final recommendations to be available in the fall of 2010.

The Semiconductor Industry Association established an Anti-Counterfeiting Task Force in June 2006, which aims to stop counterfeit semiconductors from entering the marketplace. According to the task force Chairman, its work with U.S. Customs and Border Protection led to the seizure of 1.6 million counterfeit semiconductors over the past 2 years.

Other industry associations are also focusing their efforts on mitigating the risk of counterfeit parts. Business Action to Stop Counterfeiting and Piracy has developed a clearinghouse for information about counterfeiting and piracy to facilitate information exchange.[16] The Electronic Industry Citizenship Coalition developed a risk-assessment tool for technology-industry companies to help determine the appropriate level of intensity of supplier audits and also asks suppliers about how they manage their subtier suppliers.[17] The International Anti-Counterfeiting Coalition has helped the auto industry bring 10 global manufacturers together to discuss common global counterfeiting problems, and also provides opportunities to its members to participate in training programs.[18]

The recent Department of Commerce report provided practices for managing electronic counterfeits industrywide, as well as recommendations for the U.S. government to mitigate the risk of electronic counterfeit parts. The practices for managing counterfeits included (1) provide clear, written guidance to employees on what steps to take if they suspect a part is counterfeit, (2) remove and quarantine suspected and confirmed parts from regular inventory, (3) maintain an internal database to track all suspected and confirmed counterfeit components, and (4) report suspected and confirmed counterfeit parts to industry associations and databases and to law enforcement. The department's report also stated that there is little information collected on malfunctioning and nonoperational electronic parts, which gives a false impression of supply-chain security. According to the report's findings, personnel that use parts need to file Product Quality Deficiency Reports in a timely manner to report nonworking electronic components, and if this proves to be impractical for the field units, then another system of reporting needs to be developed to facilitate information sharing. Based on its survey responses, interviews, and field visits, the Department of Commerce made seven recommendations in the areas of reporting, contract award, legal guidance, enforcement activities, data collection, information sharing, and DOD acquisition planning.

## CONCLUSION

As DOD draws from a large network of suppliers in an increasingly global supply chain, there can be limited visibility into these sources and greater risk of procuring counterfeit parts, which have the potential to threaten the reliability of DOD's weapon systems and the success of its missions. DOD needs a departmentwide definition and consistently used means for detecting, reporting, and disposing of counterfeit parts. Collaboration with government agencies, industry associations, and commercial-sector companies that produce items similar to those used by DOD and have reported taking actions to mitigate the risks of counterfeit parts in their supply chains offers DOD the opportunity to leverage ongoing and planned initiatives in this area. Some of these initiatives, such as MDA practices and industry detection and disposal processes, can be considered for DOD's immediate use. However, as DOD collects data and acquires knowledge about the nature and extent of counterfeit parts in its supply chain, additional actions may be needed to help better focus its risk-mitigation strategies.

## RECOMMENDATIONS FOR EXECUTIVE ACTION

We recommend that the Secretary of Defense take the following three actions as DOD develops its anticounterfeit program:

1. leverage existing anticounterfeiting initiatives and practices currently used by DOD components and industry to establish guidance that includes a consistent and clear definition of counterfeit parts and consistent practices for preventing, detecting, reporting, and disposing of counterfeit parts;
2. disseminate this guidance to all DOD components and defense contractors; and
3. analyze the knowledge and data collected to best target and refine counterfeit-part risk-mitigation strategies.

## AGENCY COMMENTS AND OUR EVALUATION

In written comments on a draft of this report, DOD concurred with the recommendations and identified a number of actions that it will take to address them. DOD noted that it has established teams that will leverage anticounterfeit initiatives and practices used by DOD components and industry to develop guidance by late 2010. DOD plans to include a consistent and clear definition of counterfeit parts and consistent practices for preventing, detecting, reporting, and disposing of counterfeit parts in its guidance, and plans to disseminate it to all of its components and defense contractors by early 2011. As it collects more knowledge and data on counterfeit parts, DOD plans to analyze this to best target and refine risk-mitigation strategies—which it expects to do by October 2010. According to the official leading DOD's counterfeit parts efforts, DOD will continue to refine risk-mitigation strategies on an ongoing basis as it gains more knowledge on counterfeit parts. DOD also provided technical comments, which were incorporated as appropriate. The Department of Commerce concurred with the findings in this report.

Belva Martin
Acting Director
Acquisition and Sourcing Management

## APPENDIX I: SCOPE AND METHODOLOGY

To examine the extent of the Department of Defense's (DOD) knowledge of counterfeit parts that have entered its supply chain,[1] we reviewed regulations, guidelines, and databases to determine whether they addressed how DOD should define and collect data on counterfeit parts. We met with officials from the DOD Acquisition and Technology, Logistics and Material Readiness, Supply Chain Integration office; the DOD Defense Logistics Agency and its Supply Centers located in Columbus, Ohio; Philadelphia, Pennsylvania; and Richmond, Virginia; the Army, Navy, Air Force, and Missile Defense Agency; and five defense prime contractors— BAE, Boeing, Lockheed Martin, Northrop Grumman, and Raytheon—to discuss (1) their definition of the term counterfeit,(2) their procedures and practices for obtaining knowledge of counterfeit parts, (3) databases available for documenting instances of counterfeit or suspect counterfeit parts, (4) their knowledge of the existence of counterfeit parts, and (5) instances of counterfeit parts within the DOD supply chain.

We also met with database managers from the Joint Deficiency Reporting System (JDRS), the Product Data Reporting and Evaluation Program (PDREP), and the Government Industry Data Exchange Program (GIDEP) to discuss whether these databases are able to and have been used to document instances of counterfeit or suspected counterfeit parts. Additionally, we met with officials from the Department of Commerce, Bureau of Industry and Security's Office of Technology Evaluation, to discuss their study of counterfeit electronics, which the office performed for the Navy, through the office's authority to conduct surveys and analyses and prepare reports on specific sectors of the U.S. defense supplier base.

To further examine the processes that DOD has in place to detect and prevent counterfeit parts from entering its supply chain, we conducted a case study of DOD weapon programs and interviewed program officials as well as several logistics support providers. We selected a nongeneralizable sample of

16 DOD weapon programs based on criteria including representation of the aerospace, ground vehicle, or missile defense sectors; representation of the production and deployment or operations and support phase of the acquisition life cycle, and cross-representation of DOD components—Army, Navy, Air Force, and the Missile Defense Agency. GAO also has ongoing work through its annual "Assessments of Selected Weapon Programs"[2] for many of these programs, which allowed the team to build upon our prior work efforts and existing DOD contacts. Programs selected were: F-15 Eagle, F-16 Fighting Falcon, F/A-18E/F Super Hornet, F/A-22 Raptor, C-5 Galaxy, C-130 Hercules, AH-64D Apache, UH-60 Black Hawk, E-2 Hawkeye, AV-8B Harrier, SH-60 Sea Hawk, V-22 Osprey, Aegis Cruiser, Ground-Based Midcourse Defense, High Mobility Multi-purpose Wheeled Vehicles (HMMWV), and M1 Abrams.

We identified initiatives and practices used by industry associations and commercial companies in selected commercial supply chains (electronics, automotive, aviation) to mitigate the risk of procuring counterfeit parts. We selected commercial supply chains and companies in those supply chains based on one or more of several criteria: industries in which instances of counterfeiting have taken place; companies that make products similar to DOD weapons systems in terms of complexity; and companies that make or buy products similar to those bought by DOD. We met with company officials from functions including Quality, Legal, Security, Brand Protection, and Sourcing and Supplier Management, to discuss their experiences with counterfeits (both incoming parts and counterfeit versions of their products) and processes in place to protect against counterfeits. Much of the information we obtained from these companies is anecdotal, due to the proprietary nature of the data that could affect the companies' competitive standing or level of protection against counterfeits. We visited or spoke with company officials at companies and locations including Advanced Micro Devices, Sunnyvale, California; Boeing Commercial Airplanes, Everett, Washington; Cisco Systems, Inc., San Jose, California; Federal-Mogul Corporation, Southfield, Michigan; Ford Motor Company, Dearborn, Michigan; Hewlett-Packard Company, Houston, Texas; Intel Corporation, Santa Clara, California; Meggitt Aircraft Braking Systems, Akron, Ohio; Microsoft Corporation, Redmond, Washington; and Rolls-Royce Corporation, Indianapolis, Indiana. We also met with or obtained documents from several industry associations, including the Aerospace Industries Association, Semiconductor Industry Association, Business Action to Stop Counterfeiting and Piracy, Electronic Industry Citizenship Coalition, and International Anti-Counterfeiting Coalition. We attended two counterfeit-mitigation conferences—one sponsored by DOD's Defense Standardization Program Office and the other sponsored by the Center for Advanced Life Cycle Engineering—and attended an SAE International training workshop on Aerospace Standard AS5553.

We conducted this performance audit from January 2009 to March 2010 in accordance with generally accepted government auditing standards. Those standards require that we plan and perform the audit to obtain sufficient, appropriate evidence to provide a reasonable basis for our findings and conclusions based on our audit objectives. We believe that the evidence obtained provides a reasonable basis for our findings and conclusions based on our audit objectives.

## APPENDIX II: EXAMPLES OF COUNTERFEIT PARTS IN DOD'S SUPPLY CHAIN

As shown in table 2, Department of Defense (DOD) officials that we met with provided examples of counterfeit parts. As definitions of "counterfeit" vary within DOD, the examples are based on the individual's understanding of the term; however, the examples generally refer to instances in which individuals or companies knowingly misrepresent the identity or pedigree of a part. While many of the examples are confirmed cases of counterfeit, some include cases that were not yet confirmed as the case was under investigation or the DOD official did not know the outcome.

**Table 2. Examples of Confirmed or Suspected Counterfeits in DOD's Supply Chain**

| Part | Description |
|---|---|
| Confirmed Counterfeit | |
| Electronics (confirmed) | |
| GPS receiver frequency standard oscillators | The Air Force and Navy use these oscillators on over 4,000 systems, including the Joint Surveillance Target Attack Radar System (Joint STARS). On the Joint STARS, deficient receivers could cause mission failure. An approved DOD supplier purchased the oscillators from a distributor who had used an unapproved source of supply and the problem was detected when the part had a high failure rate during depot repair. After detection, the contractor removed parts from the depot parts bin, but could not account forfive parts. Officials reported that the unaccounted-for five parts may never be found. |

| Part | Description |
|---|---|
| Confirmed Counterfeit | |
| Electronics (confirmed) | |
| Dual transistor | Multiple services commonly use this part to provide power in a system used to defeat shoulder-launched missiles. A supplier purchased the transistors from a nonfranchised distributor and detected the problem—counterfeit chips in the transistors—during routine acceptance testing and failure analysis. After detection, the supplier realized that 16 components had been shipped against the contract. The supplier paid for these 16 components to be replaced and retested. |
| Microprocessor and nonvolatile random access memory | The Air Force uses these components in the F-15 Flight Control Computer, but F-15 officials stated that the parts are in diminishing supply and difficult to procure. The microprocessors were procured from a broker, and F-15 technicians detected the problem—a falsely identified manufacturer in both cases—during repairs when they noticed additional markings on the microprocessor and character spacing inconsistent with the original part. Air Force officials stated that the parts were isolated and never released to the fleet or into supply. |
| Radar components | One of the Navy's suppliers discovered counterfeit radar components in its supply chain and worked with the Navy Criminal Investigative Service on the matter. |
| Electronic components | These components are used across services in the V-22 Osprey. Suppliers procured the parts—including fuel management units and dual digital map systems—and the problems were detected in a supply test house. |
| Microcircuit component | This microcircuit, no longer produced by the original manufacturer, is used by the Navy across a variety of platforms, including ships, airplanes, and submarines. After the Navy and its contractor purchased 75 of the microcircuits from a supplier, the Navy found that they were wired with the wrong material. Upon discovery, the parts were segregated and did not enter the supply stream. |
| Counterfeit network hardware | This hardware was purchased by multiple services and contractors and had fake labeling. Federal investigators identified nearly 3,500 counterfeit network components. |
| Operational amplifiers | The Missile Defense Agency (MDA) acquired the parts from a subcontractor who used an unauthorized distributor. MDA discovered the problem with the amplifiers while testing a circuit board. |
| Frequency synthesizer | MDA acquired a part that the supplier had acquired from an unauthorized distributor. MDA detected the problem—the surface was resurfaced and remarked—through visual inspections and authenticity testing. Investigations confirmed that a third party had tampered with the part. |
| Electronic piece parts | MDA acquired counterfeit parts used in booster and flight termination systems and detected the problem during related investigations and, in some cases, testing. |
| Fasteners (confirmed) | |

**Table 2. (Continued)**

| Part | Description |
|---|---|
| Confirmed Counterfeit | |
| Electronics (confirmed) | |
| Rotor retaining nut (used to hold the rotor to the mast of some helicopters) | The rotor retaining nut is used to hold the rotor to the mast of some helicopters; its failurewould cause the helicopter to crash. The Air Force reported that a supplier willfully supplied a substandard rotor retaining nut, but the supplier maintained its innocence and claimed that it was unaware that the part it procured was a counterfeit part. |
| Bolt | The Army reported that a bolt, intended for use in helicopters, was counterfeit. The problem was detected when Army officials recognized the serial number on the part and identified it as a defective part that had been cut in half for destruction. An X-ray test confirmed the bolt had been welded back together. |
| Hook point bolts | DLA procured this part, which is used to help stop aircraft when they land on aircraft carriers. Failure of the part could result in loss of life or aircraft. A supplier rubbed serial numbers off hooks that were too thin to use, welded additional material onto the hooks, and reused them. This problem was detected when premature part failure triggered an investigation and the welded material showed up in X-rays. |
| Packaging and labeling | |
| Hermetically-sealed microwave boxes | The Air Force reported that a contractor, who bid to repair parts, was sending them to Russia for repairs and that the resulting repairs were not done accurately. Part failure could have posed a risk to the program. |
| Other hardware | |
| Air conditioning component | Army personnel using the Bradley during operations detected a component that they suspected was counterfeit. In some climates, such as Iraq, air conditioning failure would make this vehicle inoperable and, therefore, compromise missions. Army officials were uncertain whether there was an investigation in this case. |
| Seatbelts | Army officials reported that seatbelts, provided by a supplier, were made from a cheap aluminum and were falsely certified to be the correct aluminum. The deficiency was discovered when a seatbelt part was accidentally dropped and broke. After investigation, Army investigators banned the company from selling to the Army. |

Source: GAO summary of examples provided by DOD officials.

## End Notes

[1] For purposes of this report, we are using the term "counterfeit" to refer generally to instances in which individuals or companies knowingly misrepresent the identity or pedigree of a part.

[2] SAE International is a member organization that shares information and exchanges ideas for advancing the engineering of mobility systems. SAE Aerospace Standard 5553 defines a counterfeit part as a suspect part that is a copy or substitute without legal right or authority to do so or one whose material, performance, or characteristics are knowingly misrepresented by a supplier in the supply chain.

[3] PDREP is an automated information system managed by the Navy to track quality, including part deficiencies, and is used by the Navy, DLA, the Defense Contract Management Agency (DCMA), Army ground forces, and the Marine Corps. JDRS is an automated information system that Naval Air Systems Command developed for reporting of part deficiencies for aeronautics. JDRS users include Naval Air Systems Command, Army Space and Missile Defense Command, the Air Force, the Coast Guard, and DCMA.

[4] A part that is found to be deficient is not necessarily counterfeit as counterfeit parts involve the intent to misrepresent the identity or pedigree of a part.

[5] The terms included in the list were "bogus," "counterfeit," "deliberate," "falsify," "fraud/fraudulent," "illegal," "intentional," "knowingly," "misrepresent," "piracy," and "unauthorized product substitution."

[6] The policy letter uses the term "nonconforming," which has the same meaning in DOD as the term "deficient."

[7] Department of Defense, Military Standard (MIL-STD)-1556B, Government/Industry Data Exchange Program, Contractor Participation Requirements (Feb. 24, 1986).

[8] According to the GIDEP Deputy Program Manager, this 15-day delay is in addition to the time—which can range from 30–180 days—that the DOD logistical support providers and contractors spend gathering evidence before reporting the suspect supplier to GIDEP.

[9] U.S. Department of Commerce, Defense Industrial Base Assessment: Counterfeit Electronics (Washington, D.C., January 2010). In conducting its assessment, the Department of Commerce defined a counterfeit electronic parts as one that is not genuine because it: is an unauthorized copy; does not conform to original OCM design, model, or performance standards; is not produced by the OCM or is produced by unauthorized contractors; is an off-specification, defective, or used OCM product sold as "new" or working; or has incorrect or false markings or documentation, or both.

[10] "Fake Parts are Seeping Into Military Aircraft Maintenance Depots," Inside the Air Force (Mar. 28, 2008) and "Dangerous Fakes: How Counterfeit, Defective Computer Components from China Are Getting into U.S. Warplanes and Ships," Business Week (Oct. 2, 2008).

[11] The Air Force Material Command is also developing a handbook that aims to educate its workforce on what a counterfeit part is, steps to be taken to prevent counterfeit parts from entering the supply chain, detection methods and ways to identify counterfeit parts that have already entered the supply chain, and what reporting is to be accomplished when counterfeit parts are identified. However, the command is delaying the distribution of this handbook to potentially be incorporated into a departmentwide handbook.

[12] Federal Acquisition Regulations, Part 9.103.

[13] In April 2009, SAE International issued Aerospace Standard 5553, "Counterfeit Electronic Parts; Avoidance, Detection, Mitigation and Disposition."

[14] SAE International officials told us that they plan to expand the aerospace standard to include other sectors such as the automotive industry.

[15] The Center for Advanced Life Cycle Engineering is an electronic products and systems research center focused on electronics reliability and is dedicated to providing a knowledge and resource base to support the development of competitive electronic components, products, and systems.

[16] The International Chamber of Commerce established the Business Action to Stop Counterfeiting and Piracy to take a leading role in the fight against counterfeiting.

[17] The Electronic Industry Citizenship Coalition mission is to promote an industry code of conduct for global electronics supply chains.

[18] The International Anti-Counterfeiting Coalition aims to promote enforcement standards of the intellectual property owned by its members whether copyrights, trademarks, or patents.

## End Notes for Appendix I

[1] Our review focused on DOD's knowledge of the aerospace, ground vehicle, and missile defense sectors of the defense supplier base in part given congressional interest in these sectors.

[2] GAO, Defense Acquisitions: Assessments of Selected Weapon Programs, GAO-09-326SP (Washington, D.C.: Mar. 30, 2009).

# INDEX

## A



## B



## C

## D



## E

## F



## G



## H



## I



## J



## L